D0871641

teeny, tiny cards

teeny, tiny cards

little projects that make a big impression

Jane LaFerla

LARK BOOKS
A Division of Sterling Publishing Co., Inc.
New York

Development Editor
Terry Taylor

Art Director
Susan McBride

Cover Designer
Cindy LaBreacht

Associate Art Director
Shannon Yokeley

Art Production Assistant
Jeff Hamilton

Editorial Assistance
Mark Bloom
Cassie Moore

Illustrator
Orrin Lundgren

Photographer
Keith Wright

10 9 8 7 6 5 4 3 2 1

First Edition

Published by Lark Books, A Division of
Sterling Publishing Co., Inc.
387 Park Avenue South, New York, N.Y. 10016

Library of Congress Cataloging-in-Publication Data

LaFerla, Jane.
   Teeny, tiny cards : little projects that make a big impression / Jane
LaFerla. -- 1st ed.
      p. cm.
   Includes index.
   ISBN-13: 978-1-60059-066-5 (hc-plc with jacket : alk. paper)
   ISBN-10: 1-60059-066-7 (hc-plc with jacket : alk. paper)
   1. Miniature craft. 2. Greeting cards. I. Title.
   TT178.L34 2007
   745.594'1--dc22
                                  2006101486

Distributed in Canada by Sterling Publishing,
c/o Canadian Manda Group, 165 Dufferin Street
Toronto, Ontario, Canada M6K 3H6

Distributed in the United Kingdom by GMC Distribution Services,
Castle Place, 166 High Street, Lewes, East Sussex, England BN7 1XU

Distributed in Australia by Capricorn Link (Australia) Pty Ltd.,
P.O. Box 704, Windsor, NSW 2756 Australia

If you have questions or comments about this book, please contact:
Lark Books
67 Broadway
Asheville, NC 28801
(828) 253-0467

Manufactured in China

ISBN 13: 978-1-60059-066-5
ISBN 10: 1-60059-066-7

For information about custom editions, special sales, premium and corporate
purchases, please contact Sterling Special Sales Department at 800-805-5489 or spe-
cialsales@sterlingpub.com.

contents

introduction

feeling the need for an antidote to our supersize-me world? Are you tired of multimedia, multitasking, and multitudes? Do you long to think small and have it pay off? If so, retreat to your workspace, close the door, and take a deep breath—you are about to enter an alternative, teeny, tiny universe where small is beautiful and less is more.

If you've ever been spellbound by a dollhouse or a scene inside a snow globe, you already understand the magic of miniatures. Now you can translate that same wonder into making little cards guaranteed to charm any recipient.

Twenty-two designers have created more than 40 tiny projects for this book. Using the best of today's materials and techniques, they share a range of expertise including collage, scrapbooking, stitching on paper, stamping, beading, and bookmaking. Once you get started, we know you'll be hooked.

Even though gift tags, invitations, and business cards come easily to mind when thinking of tiny cards, why stop there? Consider the impact of revealing a message bit by bit with a tiny nesting card, or the irresistible cuteness of a wee baby announcement. Then there's Valentine's Day—you can never have too many tiny hearts. And what about those photos you wanted to share? Why not make a mini-tin album!

Fold-outs, pop-ups, and puzzles lend an element of surprise to your diminutive dandies. Tiny books give your words room to ramble. A matchbox or stitched pocket provides a perfect place for concealing hidden messages. And with organza bags or tiny

tins to choose from, who needs an envelope? The possibilities are endless.

In the basics section you'll find tips for working small, and will learn how to make custom envelopes for any size card. There are easy instructions for making a simple pop-up, and by following the directions for the pamphlet stitch, you'll be making your own mini-books in no time. A special section on working with blank cards guarantees that you can have a ready-to-send card in just a few minutes.

If you're a beginner, the list of materials and tools for each project will tell you exactly what you need, and the step-by-step instructions will guide you start to finish. In the back of the book, there's a section of templates to help you complete the cards to perfection.

Projects range from simple to the more complex, so leaf through the pages, start where you feel most comfortable, and then move around at your own pace. If you're an avid cardmaker, there's a wealth of fresh ideas that will inspire your own interpretations. Or why not try a new technique? Calligraphy, polymer clay, needle work? Incorporating them into your card designs can open a whole new world of design ideas. So what are you waiting for? If you still need convincing to cross over to the small side, think of the faces of family and friends when they open one of your teeny, tiny cards. In fact, you can almost imagine their sweet chorus of *awwwwwwwwws* from here.

cardmaking
basics

While it's fun to receive cards, only you as the artist know how much more fun it is to make them. After all, you're the lucky one who gets to spend creative time playing with the materials you love. Now you can take it to a microscopic level—how low can you go? This chapter will lead you through the basic materials and supplies, tools, and techniques needed to make the cards in this book. If you've never made a card before, use the information to guide you before beginning a project. If you're an experienced paper crafter, use this information as a resource for review as needed.

a word about working small

Because you're leaving the normal-sized world to enter a miniature universe, you'll need to consider how you're going to keep all the elements of your card in proportion to one another. From the very beginning, every choice you make—whether about materials, tools, or even techniques—must be based on the smaller scale of your work.

choosing materials

When it comes to paper, you'll need to adjust the weight of the paper to suit your card's tinier dimensions. Remember that a smaller card will have shorter distances between folds and creases. If you use a paper that's too thick, stiff, or heavily textured, you'll find it difficult to manipulate while working.

Also, the thicker the paper, the thicker the folds. This may not be a problem if the card is folded once, but if you plan on multiple folds for a tiny card, you may end up with a card that's much more bulky than you want. To save frustration all around, the best advice is to always experiment with the paper before committing it to your project.

When using printed decorative papers, make sure you choose designs with smaller motifs that won't over-whelm your tiny card. That overall swirling floral pattern you loved in the store can be reduced to a disappoint-ing blob of color when cut to accommodate a small area. Likewise, if you fancy a textured paper, for example, one that imitates leather, make sure that it will still look, or "read," like leather when you cut it down to size.

The same consideration comes when selecting ephemera or other printed matter that will go on your card. If they aren't small enough to use as-is, you can take them to a copy shop and reduce them on a copier. If you're incorporating collage materials, use those that are already small or can be easily altered to fit. And don't forget text. Look for smaller alphabet stamps and stickers, and select smaller font sizes. If you don't want to buy more stamps or stickers, create your text with those you already have then use a photo-copier to reduce it to fit the size of the card.

Thanks to scrapbooking, mini-embellishments are easy to find. Whether you're looking for narrower ribbons, mini-tags, beads, charms, or novelties, such as a tiny diploma or assorted baby items, a craft store should yield results. You can also find a variety of mini-books to use. There's no bookbinding involved, and all you have to do is decorate them. However, don't discount your own ingenuity. In the heat of the creative moment, figuring out how to craft your own miniature items can open a whole new world of enjoyment.

thinking of tools

You don't need to trade in the contents of your current toolbox to make small projects. Instead, use what feels comfortable to you as you work. For instance, using a large paper cutter to cut small pieces of paper can be downright dangerous, whereas a craft knife can perform the same task in a much more manageable (and safe) way.

Whenever you're at a loss for a tool, why not improvise? The bone folder you use on larger cards may be unwieldy when fashioning a smaller one, but a tapestry needle, with its short, thick shaft and dull point, may work perfectly. Tweezers, manicure scissors, paper clips, toothpicks, cotton swabs—whatever works—can also be pressed into service when needed.

Unless your eyesight is absolutely perfect, using a magnifier—either a visor, one attached to a light, or a free-standing version—can help keep frustration at bay. And never underestimate the power of good lighting to stave off eyestrain which seems to be a natural byproduct of working small.

adjusting techniques to size

Working small takes practice and can be a technique in itself. Patience is the key. As you move down in size, techniques that might work perfectly on a larger scale can be more difficult to execute. Making adjustments to your techniques in relationship to the smaller materials you'll use will help you sail through any project. Always think in terms of ratios, such as the thickness of the paper to the number or type of folds you'll make, the amount of hot glue used to the size of the small charm it's going to affix, or the size of the beads to the depth of the envelope.

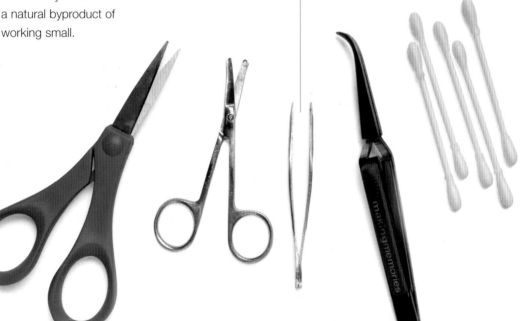

paper, cards, and envelopes

It's hard to believe that finding great papers once meant you had to go to a stationery or art supply store. Now you can find even card stock and wonderful decorative papers at your local office supply store.

Remember to think archival. It's human nature to save tiny treasures by tucking them away. As you make your cards, think of them as potential keepsakes for those who receive them and as heirlooms for future generations who find them. Whenever possible, use paper that is acid and lignin free.

the basic card

Think of the paper you'll use for your card's base, the blank card, as the canvas for your mini-masterpiece. As such, you want paper that is strong enough to stand up to the techniques you'll employ, but flexible enough to accommodate working in a smaller scale

Card stock says it all when it comes to choosing an all-purpose paper for making a card base. Its formal classification in the paper world is cover weight, which explains its function as a heavier paper when compared to paper classified as text weight, such as printer or copier paper.

Card stock is easy to find in a wide variety of textures and colors. With one quick trip to your local craft store you'll find enough to make bushels of teeny, tiny projects. A local copy shop that specializes in business cards and announcements can be another source for card stock. They may have scraps they're willing to sell

that are already cut to a smaller size—one fold and you're ready to go.

Look for other heavier weight papers for making your card base. For example, watercolor paper comes in a variety of surface textures from smooth to rough. It's made to handle any of the wet techniques, such as painting or gluing. It stands up well to tearing when creating a ragged edge and holds up when sewing.

blank cards

If you can't wait to get started with a project, use blank cards for your base. Most often made from card stock, these purchased, pre-folded cards also come with coordinating envelopes. Since you're working small, look for blank cards that are intended for use as gift enclosures or tags, small invitations, thank-you notes, and announcements. Many have the same decorative touches you find on larger blanks, such as deckle edges and embossed borders. Of course, you can always take scissors in hand and cut a larger blank card down to size, though this may leave you scrounging for an envelope to accommodate the reduced version. But no problem there—you can make one in no time. You'll find more about handmade envelopes on pages 14 and 15.

decorative papers

This is where the fun really begins. Decorative papers—commonly called scrapbooking papers—come in a limitless range of colors, and any theme you can imagine has a design on paper to match. You can use heavier weight decorative papers for your card base and the lighter ones—from text weight to tissue—for any other artistic purposes you can think of. If it's pure texture you seek, you can find papers that look like leather or fabric or those that imitate embossing or engraving.

VELLUM

This translucent paper works beautifully when you want a layered look. Though it appears delicate, it's tough enough to withstand any pounding or poking you'll do when applying brads and eyelets. Using laser-friendly vellum, you can print out text using computer fonts. This makes enticing overlays for invitations, announcements, and even recipe cards. Vellum tags ringed in metal come in smaller sizes and beg to be embellished or imprinted with text. Since water-based glue can wrinkle vellum, try using a dry adhesive such as one used for a sticker machine.

HANDMADE PAPERS

For a card that is instantly artsy, use handmade papers. Their textures and colors are irresistible—and who among you doesn't already have a sizable stash? Heavier weights make a great card base while the thinner papers can add lovely touches anywhere you want. Because this paper is handcrafted, it's generally more expensive than commercial papers.

PHOTOS, EPHEMERA, AND COLLAGE MATERIAL

What better way to personalize a card then by using photos, ephemera, or collage materials that have meaning for the recipient? These can include text from old books, postage stamps, ticket stubs, bits of dress patterns, manufactured greeting cards, postage stamps, or snippets from travel brochures. Be aware that commercially printed materials, such as those from magazines or newspapers, are not acid free.

envelopes

There's something to be said about the careful opening of an envelope with a letter opener. But ripping into an envelope to get to the surprise inside is one of the best parts of receiving a card. Though it may be tossed aside and forgotten in the heat of the moment, never underestimate the added anticipation and enjoyment a perfect envelope can bring to the overall card experience.

PURCHASED ENVELOPES

When you buy blank cards, even the tiniest ones come with envelopes. And if you make a card but don't want to make an envelope, a little extra sleuthing at a craft store or beyond can yield small envelopes in a range of shapes, colors, and materials. "Push the envelope" to find alternatives to the norm, such as those used for stamps or coins. Look for envelopes with interesting fasteners beyond the basic lick-and-stick variety. And don't be afraid to add your own special touches to a humdrum envelope. Try rubber stamping, collage, even making your own sealing stickers to provide a preview of what's inside.

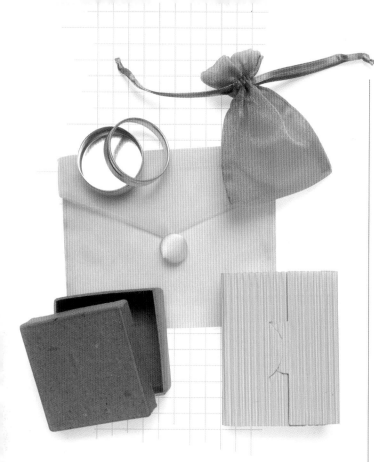

HANDMADE ENVELOPES

At some point you'll need or want to make an envelope. Either the card is too small (or too precious) to be enclosed in a purchased one, or your newly embellished blank card is no longer worthy of the plain envelope that came with it.

You can find envelope templates at craft stores or through the Internet. You can also easily make your own pattern by taking apart any envelope you fancy and tracing around it on a flat sheet of paper. A real easy way to make a template is to take an envelope apart, lay it on the glass platen of a photocopier, and then cover it with dark paper before copying. The copy will have

figure 1

You can also abandon the traditional concept of envelope altogether. Try using small organza bags to create a unique presentation. If your card is highly embellished, you may need to find a small box to accommodate its extra depth. Recycled containers also work well. Matchboxes and small candy tins provide both a novel and practical way to present thicker cards.

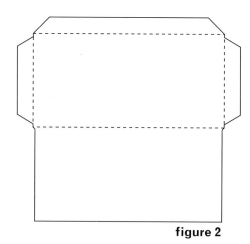

figure 2

an outline that's a snap to cut. You'll find that some projects in the book provide patterns for envelopes, which are included at the back of the book.

The basic rule of thumb for making an envelope is that the center rectangle or square should be 1/8 to 3/8 inches (3mm to 1cm) larger than the card. The pattern in figure 1 is for a standard envelope; figures 2 and 3 are alternative designs. Try experimenting with elongated or rounded flaps for a custom look.

Once you decide on the shape, use a bone folder to score and fold (see page 21) the two side flaps in and the bottom flap up. After making sure the folds are nice and sharp, glue the bottom flap in place. You can use double-stick tape to seal the envelope, or try using a sticker or sealing wax and seal for a novel closure.

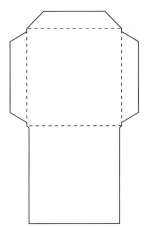

figure 3

mailing matters

Think before tossing your precious piece of mail art into the nearest mail box. Its smaller-than-standard size may delay delivery and can cost more for postage. Knowing a few facts can help get your card to its destination in a timely manner.

* Learn your postal service's size and shape requirements for standard-size letters and postcards.
* Unusually shaped or small cards weighing one ounce or less are more difficult to process because they can jam postal equipment. As such, they may be subject to a surcharge to cover special handling.
* Envelopes and postcards that are highly decorated, or those made of slippery or highly textured paper, can stall sorting machinery.
* Envelopes that are dark in color, such as navy blue or black, will interfere with the scanning equipment that reads postal bar codes.
* An overweight card in a bulging envelope is just as difficult to process as one that is thinner than a standard postcard.
* Sharp objects affixed to cards or broken pieces from fragile embellishments that are damaged in handling can poke through the envelope and damage postal machinery.

If you have any doubts about the mail-ability of your card, the simplest solution is to take it to the nearest post office where you can ask about proper handling. Be mindful that there's no disgrace in placing your tiny envelope inside a larger one. Not only will it keep it safe for delivery, it will delightfully prolong the suspense for the recipient.

tools

Ruler. Scissors. Craft knife. The basic tools for making a card are few. If you're starting out, you probably have most of the tools needed to make the cards in this book. As you work, you may want to look for tools that will make some of the more repetitive tasks easier, or for specialized tools designed to add a decorative touch.

AWL

This small pointed tool comes in handy for punching holes in paper prior to hand stitching. You may find that placing the paper on a piece of foam core or corrugated card-board before punching will make the job easier.

BONE FOLDER

Made of bone, wood, or resin, this bookbinding tool is essential for scoring paper and making sharp creases when folding.

BRUSHES

If your card involves painting, make sure you have a good selection of brushes on hand that are suited to the type of paint you're using. For applying glue, use inexpensive, flat, synthetic bristle brushes with water-based liquid adhesives, including decoupage medium. Always keep your paint and glue brushes separate.

CRAFT KNIFE

This tool is indispensable for making small accurate cuts. The disposable blades come in all shapes and sizes. Remember to keep plenty of fresh blades on hand since a dull blade will make ragged edges.

CUTTING MAT

When using a craft knife, always place the paper on a self-healing cutting mat. The surface of the mat protects the knife's blade and keeps the paper from curling, and the mat's measuring grid conveniently keeps track of small dimensions.

DECORATIVE-EDGE SCISSORS

Take a test cut before using—this is one place to consider scale. For example, scissors made to cut a scalloped edge on a regular-sized card may only produce one or two scallops on your tinier version.

EYELET-SETTING TOOL

This specialized tool allows you to affix eyelets to cards. With a quick tap of the hammer, the tool rolls the metal of the eyelet down to hold it in place. Following the manufacturer's instructions will bring you instant success.

PUNCHES

The wide range of patterns available in shaped punches brings unlimited design potential to your cards. Always look for shaped punches that will make smaller motifs in line with the scale of your cards. You can use a traditional hole punch to make circles, but don't forget that you can find simple circle punches in a wide variety of sizes, including those that will make the tiniest of holes.

RULER AND SQUARES

A cork-back metal ruler provides a smooth, pit-resistant edge for guiding your craft knife, while the cork keeps the ruler from slipping. Use an L-square or T-square to ensure sharp angles when cutting larger sheets of paper.

SCISSORS

Choose scissors by size for the task at hand. Long-bladed scissors will cut large paper down to size, but if you need to trim around small motifs or are clipping tiny corners, think about using a pair with short blades. You might find that a pair of straight-blade, not curved, manicure scissors are just what you need.

SEWING TOOLS

Hand or machine stitching on cards is a *hot* trend— and yields beautiful results. Always make sure the needles you use are sharp. When hand stitching, you want the needle to glide effortlessly through the paper to avoid ragged tears or wrinkling. You may want to use a slightly larger needle or an awl to punch holes in the paper first, and then follow with the thinner needle and thread. When stitching paper on a machine, select a sharp needle in a size that will accommodate the thicknesses of the paper and fabric you are using.

TAPE

Little pieces of paper waiting to be used are notorious for catching the slightest breeze and blowing off your work surface. Low-tack tape, which leaves no residue, can hold them in place until you're ready for them. And if you're looking to create a dimensional effect, double-sided foam tape will give elements the lift they need to stand away from the paper.

Materials

If you think of making cards as following a recipe, paper will always be the main ingredient, with glue in second place. After that, add whatever is needed to fulfill your creative vision and spice-up your design.

ADHESIVES

There are many different varieties of adhesives, a.k.a. glue, you can use when making cards. Common white craft glue—polyvinyl acetate, or PVA—is perfect for general purposes. Using a toothpick to apply the glue rather than squeezing it from the bottle will give you more control. Glue sticks and glue pens work well for adhering smaller pieces since they allow you to apply just the right amount exactly where you want it.

If you're embellishing the card with objects such as beads or charms, use tacky craft glue which is thicker than PVA and dries clear. Spray adhesive is particularly handy when working with thin strips of paper or fabric since it won't spill or leak over the edges of the pieces to be glued.

Decoupage medium, which you can find in any craft store, will glue an image to your card and seal it at the same time. You can also make your own medium by thinning white glue with a little bit of water.

Hot glue is a handy and strong adhesive, but also can be used to create an easy dimensional effect. First, use the hot glue to draw designs on your card, and then after the glue dries, simply paint over it.

And don't forget one of the best scrapbooking inventions ever. A sticker machine applies adhesive to paper, images, or cut shapes, allowing you to make stickers out of just about anything you can feed into it.

BEADS AND BUTTONS

If you love beads and buttons, you've probably figured out by now how to incorporate them into everything you make. When adding them to cards, stitch or glue them in place or affix them with wire. Keep your ratios in mind, selecting small beads and buttons that will match the proportions of the card.

BRADS AND EYELETS

Why glue photos or papers to your cards when there are so many other decorative alternatives for attaching them? Once an office supply staple, brads now come in an array of colors, shapes, and sizes. Eyelets, easily affixed with a few quick taps on an eyelet tool, can also add visual interest and texture to any attachment.

FOUND OBJECTS AND NATURAL MATERIALS

Found objects can add a quirky twist to your card's design. You'll be surprised how buttons, washers, bottle caps, or even pieces of old jewelry can enhance the idea you're trying to convey. Natural materials—such as leaves, feathers, or pressed flowers—will add emotional texture to a card.

METAL ACCESSORIES

If you want to add shine and/or visual interest to your cards, think about using foil, wire, or metal sheets. You can twist the wire to make interesting embellishments, or incise the metal sheets for an embossed look. Using metal mesh can also bring new dimensions to your card.

PAINT

Over time you've undoubtedly collected bottles, tubes, and cakes of various types of paint. Water-based acrylic is a good all-purpose craft paint since it mixes well, dries fast, and cleans up with water.

PENS, PENCILS, AND MARKERS

Rely on the variety these writing and drawing implements offer. From colored pencils to glitter pens, they will add interest to your lettering or drawing.

POLYMER CLAY

If you can't find the exact little trinket or bead you need for your card, fashion it yourself from polymer clay. Before baking the clay to harden it, you can apply texture to the surface of the object or stamp it with an initial or name to personalize it.

STAMPING INKS

When using stamps, standard dye-based inks—the kind found in most inkpads—work well on coated papers. When working on papers that are uncoated or more absorbent, such as card stock, use pigment inks. Though they dry more slowly than dye-based inks, their opaque quality and thicker texture will produce more satisfactory results.

STAMPS

These incredibly versatile tools are a mainstay of card-makers. Store-bought stamps abound, or try making your own by cutting your design into an eraser.

Whatever stamp you use, remember to keep its image in scale to your card.

THREADS

Basic embroidery floss works well when hand stitching on cards. For a more sophisticated look, consider using waxed linen thread. When machine stitching, anything goes—as long as it will sew material, it will work on paper. If you're attaching beads, make sure to use single-strand nylon beading thread which is strong enough to ensure that the beads will stay where you want them.

SCRAPBOOKING MATERIALS

This may be the shortcut you're looking for. Many embellishments made for scrapbooking are already the size you need. From stencils to stickers, from trinkets to text, look in the scrapbooking aisle of any craft store for instant inspiration.

SLIDE MOUNTS

Used to keep slide film in place, slide mounts are perfectly sized for working small. They're great for framing photos or images and beg to be decorated and embellished.

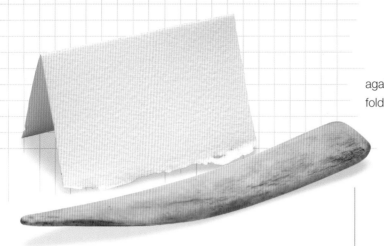

against that line while running the sharp point of a bone folder along the edge of the ruler.

Fold the card along the scored line. Use the curved side of the bone folder to press the paper flat at the fold—and you're ready to go!

techniques

Cut. Fold. Glue. Any questions? Yes, it's really that easy to make a card. In a few minutes you can master the basic techniques for making your blank card. Then it's on to the art part—learning all the fun techniques you need for decorating and embellishing it.

cutting, scoring, and folding

Before you take the first cut, determine the size of your finished card. For a simple card with one fold, trim the paper to twice its finished size, which allows for a front and back panel. For cards with multiple folds, multiply the finished size by the number of folds you'll make.

If you're ever in doubt about sizing, use a piece of scrap paper to make a prototype of the card, and then, when satisfied, use it as a pattern for cutting. And, whether you use a paper trimmer or craft knife for cutting the card, make sure your cuts are clean and neat.

Always score the card before folding it. Scoring breaks the top fibers in the paper to ensure an even fold exactly where you want it. To score your card, first use a ruler and pencil to mark your fold line on the side of the paper that will fall inside the card. Then hold the ruler

going with the grain

Just as the phrase "going with the grain" cautions us to take the path of least resistance, it also provides good advice when working with paper. Most manufactured paper and some handmade papers have a grain, which is the way the fibers line up on the sheet. Tearing or folding paper *with* the grain, meaning *parallel* to it, is the way to avoid resistance that can lead to imperfect folds or even ragged breaks.

✳ To find the grain, fold a sheet of paper either top to bottom or side to side. Do not crease it. When the paper is folded with the grain, the curve of the fold will look flatter and feel softer than when folded against the grain.

✳ If you're making a card with multiple folds, always fold with the grain in order to achieve crisp creases which produce a flatter card. This is especially important when working small, and will help you avoid adding any excess thickness. Keep in mind that most handmade papers do not have a grain, making them less predictable when it comes time to cut and fold.

gluing

If you've never given much thought to gluing, here's your chance to get it right. When working small, applying glue exactly where it needs to go is crucial—it's much easier to clean up or disguise gluing mistakes on large surfaces than on small ones.

Start by applying the glue to the material you're going to adhere to the card rather than vice versa. This gives you much better control over the amount of glue to use and helps you avoid those globs of excess glue that ooze out from underneath the applied materials. When gluing tiny components to your card, you may need to use the tip of a craft knife or tweezers to position them accurately.

Always allow any glue to dry thoroughly. To provide maximum adhesion when gluing flat pieces— those without dimensional elements or components— and to ensure that the paper will not curl as the glue dries, press the cards overnight under a pile of heavy books.

decorating and embellishing

Up until now you've been learning about the tools, materials, and techniques you'll use for making cards. Now it's time to take that information and apply it to creating cards that reflect your own individual style. This section discusses popular design techniques you can use to achieve the cards you envision. You can use one technique on a card or mix and match them as much as you dare.

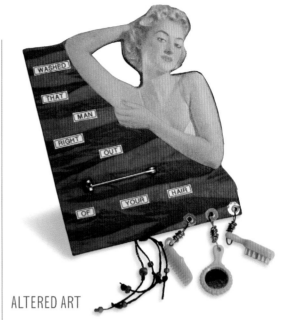

ALTERED ART

With altered art, an artist starts with an object and changes (alters) it in such a way that challenges the viewer's conventional way of looking at it. Some materials that can be altered for use in small cards can be old postcards, bits of dress patterns, old game pieces and cards, small charms and bits of jewelry, bottle caps, and text or pictures from old books.

BOOKMAKING

Imagine the surprise in finding a small book tucked into a tiny pocket of a card? Or, the potential of expanding your message with a simple, small accordion book? Incorporating basic bookmaking into your designs can enhance your cards. Several projects in this book borrow these techniques.

One of the most basic ways to make a small book is to use the easy pamphlet stitch to hold the pages together (see figure 4). Stitch, loop, and tie—that's all there is to it. Insert the needle

figure 4

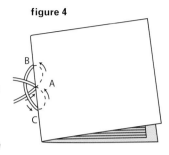

at point A, leaving a tail of thread, and then bring the needle out at point B. Take the needle through point C and out again at point A. Check that the long stitch between points B and C is in between the ends of the tail before tying the knot in the tail to finish. For easier sewing through several thicknesses, you may want to pierce the holes first with an awl or larger needle before following with your regular needle and thread.

COLLAGE

Collage is a way to recombine materials to create a whole new pattern. Employing the simple technique of cut and paste, you mix and layer textures and colors—a process that can be very freeing. Keep a variety of papers and fabrics at hand, and then let the moment seize you.

USING THE COMPUTER AND PHOTOCOPIER

Don't underestimate the use of the computer, printer, and photocopier when making tiny cards. A word processing program and Internet access will bring millions of fonts to your fingertips, allowing you to create text that you can print as small as your card requires. If you have a photo-editing program, you can manipulate images, colorize them, miniaturize them, and print them at will. With an illustration program, you can combine different effects to design your card on the screen, then print it to the exact size you desire.

You can also achieve interesting variations by experimenting with printing on different papers. Printer-friendly vellum can open you to a world of artistic overlays. Try creating your own photo transfers by printing on paper manufactured for that purpose.

Photocopying gives you the ability to copy and reduce the size of ephemera that would otherwise be too big for a tiny card. If you have artwork that you've already made and would like to use on a tiny card, simply copy a smaller version and you're ready to go. You can also compose designs directly on the copier by layering materials and images—this can be great fun and is well worth the experimentation.

MIXED MEDIA

If you're wondering what mixed media is, think salad. It's using a combination of bits and pieces of different media rather than limiting yourself to one medium. For example, if you make a card that is painted, has fabric sewn to it, and is embellished with buttons, you've made a mixed-media card.

POP-UPS

If you love pop-ups, don't discount using them in your tiny cards. Space restrictions may dictate that they be less elaborate than you want, but keep in mind they will nonetheless enchant the recipient.

figure 5

figure 6

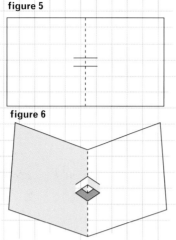

To make a simple pop-up, you need to cut a tab inside the card. Start with a folded card, open it, and lay it flat. You want the tab at the center of the card. Measure down from the top and make one mark on the fold, and then measure down from the first mark and make another. The distance between marks determines the width of the tab. Using the marks as your guide, draw two parallel lines that extend from either side of the center fold, as shown in figure 5. The length of the lines determines the length of the tab. Use a craft knife to cut through the lines, and then fold the tab out at its center point, as shown in figure 6, which will allow the card to fold flat. Adhere whatever you want to the tab for your pop-up.

SCRAPBOOKING

When you make cards, it's hard to ignore the influence scrapbooking has had on paper crafts in general. For example, scrapbooking has elevated layering and embellishment to art. Borrowing these popular techniques and materials when making cards will open many design possibilities. The use of brads, eyelets, overlays, and clever ways to attach photos to paper can enhance your card designs. Best of all, scrapbooking materials tend to be on the small side—a definite plus when making tiny cards.

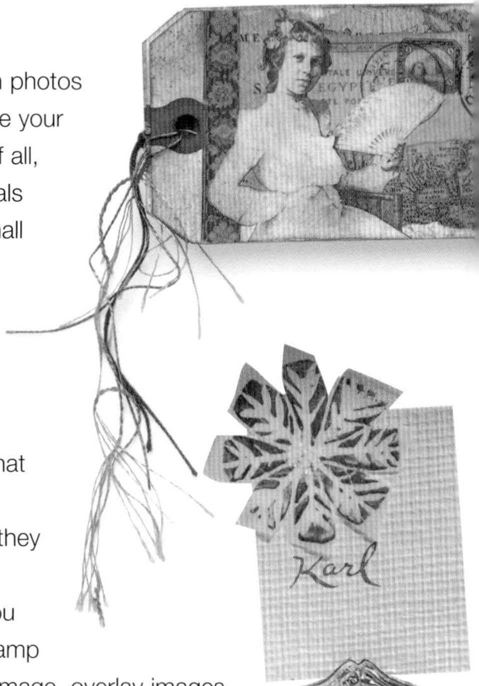

STAMPING

Aside from the fact that stamps allow you to reproduce a design, they can be a tool in the hands of an artist. You can use the same stamp to imprint a singular image, overlay images, or print partial images. And used in the context of a collage or mixed media design, a stamp can create a totally different look. Alphabet stamps, which come in a wide variety of fonts, allow you to add text or personalize a card.

STITCHING AND BEADING

Even if you don't sew or embroider like a pro, consider incorporating stitching on your cards. The stitches can be purely decorative or functional when used to hold other elements to the paper. The incredible variety of threads available—from homespun fibers to slick metallics—will suit any style. If you've sewn a hem, you have all the know-how you need to hand stitch a border or sprinkle a card with stitches.

If you have needle and thread in hand anyway, why not add beads? They're guaranteed to add textural interest and sparkle whether they complement a design or stand on their own as a focal element. Beads can also be affixed with wire or glued to the cards.

For more complex designs, drag out the old sewing machine, thread it, and see where it leads. Machine sewing is a perfect way to layer paper or fabric on your cards. You don't have to confine yourself to sewing a straight line—turn the paper as you work or mix and match stitches at will.

calling cards

In Victorian times, presenting a calling card when paying a social visit was strictly *de rigueur*. The rigid social rules of the day dictated exactly who sent what to whom and precisely when, where, and how it was proper to do so.

✱ Calls between three and four in the afternoon were limited to visits concerning condolences, births, and marriage. Calls between five and six were strictly intended for more intimate purposes.

✱ Men could present their wives' cards, but wives could not present their husbands'. And, if you failed to receive a formal response to presenting your card, it was an indication that any anticipated relationship would not go forward.

✱ While antique calling cards are quite collectable, a new wave of interest in this social custom has surfaced in the form of handcrafted calling cards. These small works of art, exchanged in much more relaxed and lenient circumstances, are becoming a popular, creative way to announce one's presence any time of day.

✱ Business cards can be considered today's calling cards. Everyone seems to have one— the trick is making yours stand out from the rest. While anyone can print out cards on their home computer and printer, nothing is more intriguing than singular cards made to show off your handiwork. You'll find inspiration for making your own on pages 44, 68, 78, 96, and 110.

the beauty of the blank

Drawing a blank when you're at a loss for a card idea may not be as bad as it seems. If you're looking for quick inspiration, start with a package of purchased blank cards, assemble your favorite materials, and see where your creativity leads you. With a sleight of creative hand, designer Terry Taylor shows you how you can transform a humble 3- x 3-inch (7.6 x 7.6 cm) blank into an array of beautiful and unique cards.

✳ HOLIDAY SPIRIT

I had a sheet of vintage lithographic Santas waiting to be used. The sheet didn't have an adhesive backing, but a quick run through the sticker machine fixed that. I punched a shape in the front panel, adhered one of the Santa stickers to clear acetate, then adhered the acetate to the inside of the card to complete the window. Foil on the back panel added holiday sparkle, along with punched-foil embellishments.

designer: terry taylor

✳ SPARKLING DAISIES

The printed vellum with glitter highlights imparted a muted orange tone when adhered to the front of the card. I used tiny punched flowers to highlight the paper's subtle daisy pattern. Although the blank cards came with envelopes, I couldn't resist making a matching one from the vellum.

✳ WISH YOU WERE HERE

This card is the easiest of all. Use small, round rubber stamps that imitate postmarks to create the background. Then apply a canceled stamp to complete the theme.

the projects

Pick a card, any card. The following pages are full of tiny card ideas that are as fun to make as they are to give.

beads
& organza

Dressed in glittering beads and shimmering organza,
this little gem of a card can become a keepsake place
setting or a truly memorable thank-you note.

size:
card,
1½ x 1½ inches
(3.8 x 3.8 cm);
bag,
3 x 3 ½ inches
(7.6 x 8.9 cm)

materials

Solid-color card stock

Rubber stamp
with colored ink pad

Scrap pieces of card
stock in coordinating colors

Glue

Beading thread

Seed beads and
small decorative beads

Sheer fabric bag with
ribbon tie

tools

Scissors

Ruler

Pencil

Bone folder

Decorative circle punches

Beading needle

process

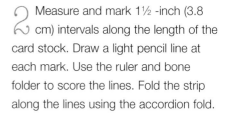

1 Cut a piece from the solid-color card stock measuring 1½ x 7½ inches (3.8 x 19.3 cm). Stamp one side of the strip, allow it to dry, then repeat on the other side. Note: When stamping, leave some blank space on the card stock for a written message.

2 Measure and mark 1½ -inch (3.8 cm) intervals along the length of the card stock. Draw a light pencil line at each mark. Use the ruler and bone folder to score the lines. Fold the strip along the lines using the accordion fold.

3 Use the punches to make circles from scraps of solid-color card stock. Use glue to adhere them to the cover of the card. Note: Allowing some of the circles to extend off the edges of the card creates a nice effect. Once you adhere the circles, trim their edges flush with the card.

4 Use the needle and thread to sew a selection of beads to the card, passing the needle and thread through the cover. Follow the curve of each circle to highlight its shape.

5 Place your card inside the fabric bag, and pull the ribbons to close.

collage
gift cards

size:

{ 1⅝ x 2 inches
(4.1 x 5 cm) }

These tiny beauties are perfect for smaller presents.
You can make them in any color combination to complement the
package they'll adorn. Decorate the front to your heart's content,
but don't forget to leave the inside blank for your message.

materials

Card stock

Decorative paper in vintage designs

Text from vintage books

Decoupage medium

Glue

Ribbon

tools

Scissors

Pencil

Bone folder

Glue brush

Hole punch

Tweezers

process

1 Cut the card stock to size. Note: The card stock used for this project was purchased precut to business-card size.

2 Mark the fold line lightly with a pencil. Score the line using a bone folder. Fold the card stock in half.

3 Decorate the front panel of the card using vintage-design papers and text from vintage books. Adhere them with glue or use a brush and decoupage medium.

4 Punch a hole in the corner of the card and attach a piece of ribbon.

designer: sharon wisely

all treats, no trick party invites & favors

Grab your costume—it's time for trick or treat. From invitations to favors, you'll have the makings for one great party.

size:

Invitation, 2¼ x 3½ inches (5.7 x 8.9 cm); screen favor, 1½ x 3½ inches (3.8 x 8.9 cm); pin with clip, 1 x 2 inches (2.5 x 5.1 cm)

materials

Black acrylic paint

Metal Halloween charm

#200-grit sandpaper

Rubber stamps with Halloween images

Black ink pad

Orange and white polka dot paper

Black paper tags, 1¼ x 2¾ inches (3.2 x 7 cm) and 2 x 3½ inches (5.1 x 8.9 cm)

Stick-on gem (optional)

Alphabet stamps or stickers

Orange paper

Glue

Metal-edged circle tags

Circle slide mount

Coin envelopes

Metal screening

Black eyelets

Black and white polka dot paper

Gold polka dot paper

Ribbon

Button

Bottle caps

Glitter

Tiny black clips

Tiny orange pompons

tools

Small paintbrush

Scissors

Computer and printer (optional)

Circle punches, 1-inch (2.5 cm) and 2-inch (5.1 cm)

Die cutter (optional)

Eyelet-setting tool

invitations

process

1 Paint the metal charm with black acrylic paint. Allow to dry, and then lightly sand with the sandpaper to distress.

2 Rubber stamp a Halloween image on orange and white polka dot paper. Cut the stamped image to fit on a 2 x 3½ inch (5.1 x 8.9 cm) black paper tag. Glue the image to the front of the tag.

3 If desired, attach the metal charm at the tag's string hole and adhere a stick-on jewel to the image.

4 Rubber stamp an invitation on orange paper and glue it to the back of the black tag. You can use alphabet stamps or stickers for your text, or you can use a computer to generate text and print it out.

envelopes

1 Rubber stamp a Halloween image onto orange and white polka dot paper. Then use a 1-inch (2.5 cm) circle punch to punch out the image.

2 Paint a 1-inch (2.5 cm) metal-edged circle tag with black acrylic paint. Distress the dried paint lightly with the sandpaper. Glue the stamped circle made in step 1 to the distressed tag.

3 Glue a black-plastic circle slide mount to the front of the coin envelope. Glue the distressed, stamped circle tag to the envelope, positioning it in the center of the slide mount.

4 Cut the flap off the envelope. Use the 1-inch (2.5 cm) circle punch to punch a half circle at the top of the envelope.

Variation Rubber stamp a Halloween image onto orange and white polka dot paper, and then use a 2-inch (5.1 cm) circle punch to punch it out. Paint a 2-inch (5.1 cm) metal-edged circle tag with black acrylic paint and distress with sandpaper. Glue the stamped image to the tag before gluing it to the envelope.

screen favor

1 Paint the screen with black acrylic paint and allow to dry. Die cut a coin envelope out of the painted screen. You can also use a disassembled coin envelope as a template for cutting the screen. Fold the envelope, and set an eyelet at the bottom edge.

2 Cover a 1¼- x 2¾-inch (3.2 x 7 cm) paper tag with the black and white polka dot paper. Rubber stamp a Halloween image onto gold polka dot paper, trim the paper to fit, and glue onto the tag.

3 Thread the ribbon through the button, tying it with a simple overhand knot to secure. Glue the button to the top of the tag. Insert the tag into the screen envelope.

clip-on pin

1 Flatten a bottle cap and paint it with black acrylic paint. Sprinkle glitter on the wet paint and allow to dry.

2 Rubber stamp a Halloween image onto orange and white polka dot paper. Punch out the stamped image using a 1-inch (2.5 cm) circle punch. Glue the stamped circle to the bottle cap.

3 Tie an orange ribbon to a tiny black clip. Glue a pompom onto the clip. Attach the clip to the bottle cap.

designer: terry taylor

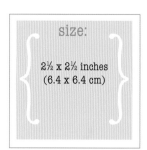

it's a ...

The pastel colors of wee coin envelopes inspired these pop-up cards. Make them to use for gift cards or as one-of-a-kind birth announcements.

materials

Card stock

Vintage images

Decorative paper

Glue stick

Coin envelopes

Decorative lettering

Vellum

tools

Photocopier

Sticker machine

Pencil

Ruler

Bone folder

Craft knife

process

1 Make a simple folded card from card stock that will fit inside the envelope you've chosen.

2 Select an image you wish to use for your pop-up. The designer chose images from vintage illustrated children's dictionaries. Photocopy the images and, if needed, reduce them in size to fit within the dimensions of the card. Make multiple copies, run them through a sticker machine, and adhere them to card stock for strength.

3 To make the tab for the pop-up, follow the directions for making a simple pop-up on page 24. Make a mark 1 inch (2.5 cm) down from the top. Make another mark ½ inch (1.3 cm) down from that. Using the marks as your guide, draw two parallel lines that extend ¼ inch (1.3 cm) from either side of the center fold making each line ¼ inch (1.3 cm) long. Use the craft knife to cut the lines.

4 Cut a piece of decorative paper the same size as the opened card or slightly larger. Use a glue stick to spread adhesive on the outside of the card stock. Be very careful to avoid getting any adhesive on the tab. Adhere the decorative paper to the card. Trim as needed.

5 Cut out the image mounted on card stock in step 2. Apply a small amount of glue to the tab, and then attach the image.

6 Use decorative lettering to write your chosen message on the card. Decorate the front of the envelope as desired.

Tip To make the pop-up surprise even more so, tease the recipient by prolonging the suspense. Use a blue envelope for a girl and a pink one for a boy, placing the text, "It's a..." on the outside.

sewn collage cards

Who needs a plan? Get out the sewing machine, take a blank card, add metallic threads and decorative papers, and let the creativity flow.

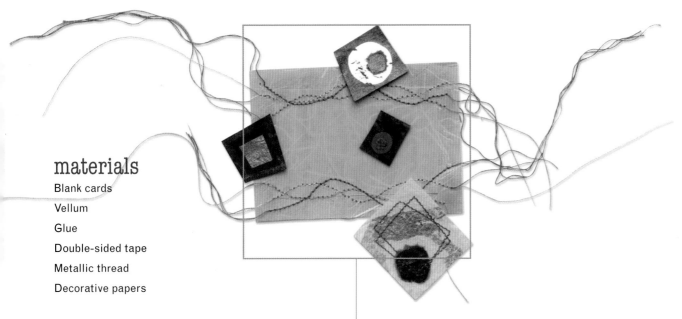

materials

Blank cards

Vellum

Glue

Double-sided tape

Metallic thread

Decorative papers

tools

Tools

Scissors

Ruler

Sewing machine

process

1 Cut rectangles from vellum that are slightly smaller than the front of the card. Position a vellum rectangle on a card and adhere it to the front with glue or double-sided tape.

2 Using the sewing machine and metallic thread, stitch over the vellum as desired. Have fun running the paper through the machine—make wavy lines on some or outline the vellum at unusual angles on others. If desired, leave threads untrimmed to extend off the edges of the card.

3 Cut or tear small shapes from decorative paper and adhere them to the front of the card around the edges of the vellum.

4 Cut squares and rectangles from decorative paper. Group a few as you would when piecing a patchwork quilt, and then stitch them together on the sewing machine. Don't trim the threads close after sewing. Long threads extending from the edges will add textural interest. Adhere the patchwork piece to the back of the card. If desired, adhere small shapes that have been cut or torn from decorative papers to the patchwork.

5 You can use this card two ways. Use the vellum side for place cards, or turn the card over to use it as a greeting with the patchwork on the front.

size:

{ 2 x 2½ inches
(5.1 x 6.4 cm) }

anniversary invitation

Though small, this invitation holds a lifetime of memories.
The vintage snapshot sets the mood for raising a champagne
toast to the couple at their anniversary brunch.

materials

Black card stock

Photo

Sandpaper

Vintage ribbon

Glue

Parchment paper

Bird charm

Acrylic paint, white

tools

Scissors

Bone folder

Craft knife

Scallop-edge scissors

Computer and printer

Small paintbrush

process

1 Cut a 2½- x 4-inch (6.4 x 10.2 cm) piece of black card stock. Use the bone folder to score and fold the paper in half to the make the card. Repeat for the amount of invitations needed.

2 If necessary, photocopy or print multiple images for the front panel. Reduce or enlarge the image as needed. Trim the photo to fit the front of the invitation. Use the decorative scissors to trim the bottom edge of the image. Distress the edges of the photo by sanding lightly with the sandpaper.

3 Tear a strip of vintage ¾-inch-wide (1.9 cm) ribbon approximately 16 inches (40.6 cm) long. Position the ribbon on the front of the card with its ends extending from the edges of the paper. Glue the photo on top of the ribbon

4 Generate the text for the invitation on the computer and print it on white parchment paper. Trim the parchment to fit, using the scallop-edge scissors to trim the right-hand side. Glue the text sheet inside the card.

5 Paint a metal bird charm with white acrylic paint and glue it to the inside of the invitation. Tie the vintage ribbon in a bow, and the invitation is ready for mailing or delivery.

designer: sharon wisely

we eloped!
announcement

Looking for unique ways to tell friends and family about out-of-the-ordinary events can be lots of fun. Could a luggage tag be any more perfect for announcing an elopement?

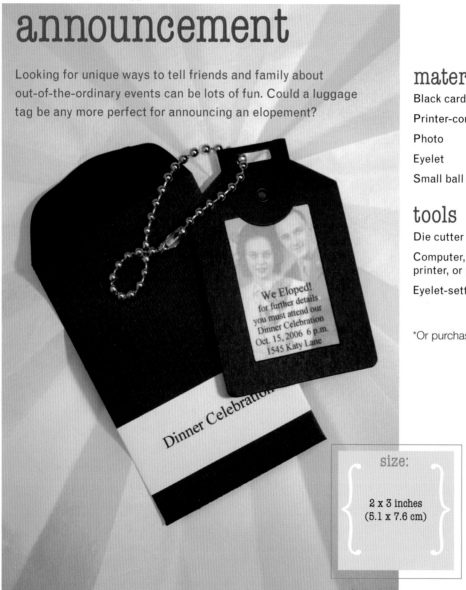

We Eloped!
for further details
you must attend our
Dinner Celebration
Oct. 15, 2006 6 p.m.
1545 Katy Lane

Dinner Celebration

materials

Black card stock*

Printer-compatible vellum

Photo

Eyelet

Small ball chain

tools

Die cutter

Computer, photo-editing software, printer, or photocopier

Eyelet-setting tool

*Or purchased paper luggage tag

size:
2 x 3 inches
(5.1 x 7.6 cm)

process

1 Die cut a luggage tag from black card stock. You may be able to find a novelty paper tag used in scrapbooking.

2 Use the computer to generate your text. Make sure the text, when printed, will fit in the tag's window and that it will be positioned where you want it to be over the photo. Print the text on printer-compatible vellum.

3 Trim a photo to fit inside the luggage tag. If necessary, use photo-editing software or a photocopier to reduce or enlarge the size of the photo.

4 Slip the photo into the tag's window, and then overlay it with the printed vellum. If needed, use the eyelet-setting tool to attach an eyelet when assembling the tag.

5 Attach a small silver ball chain to the luggage tag.

6 Make a simple envelope for the tag. Insert the tag into the envelope, allowing the chain to act as the pull for getting it out.

designer: margert kruljac

creative shapes business card

If you're all about art, why hide it? These creative cards will leave no doubt about your artistic intentions.

size:

3½ x 2 inches
(8.9 x 5.1 cm)

materials

Orange card stock

Decorative
coordinating papers

Glue

Printer-compatible
transparency sheets

Decorative brads

Stick-on letters

tools

Scissors

Sewing Machine

Computer and printer

Shaped punches for
circles, triangles,
or rectangles

Sticker machine

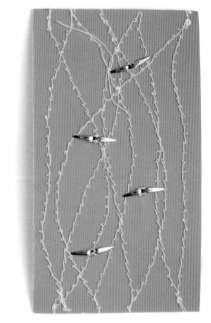

process

1 Cut the card stock and decorative paper to the
same size. Glue the decorative paper to the
card stock, tearing its edges in a random fashion
to allow the card stock to peek through. Allow to
dry before machine stitching at random over the
entire card.

2 Use the art function of your word processing
program to format your text in circles, rectangles,
or triangles. Manipulate the shapes until they're the size
you desire. Print the formatted text on
printer-compatible transparency
sheets.

3 Use the punches to cut circles,
triangles, or rectangles from
coordinating decorative paper.
Vary the size of the punches if
desired. As shown in the card
with the circles, a larger punch
was used for the name, the same
size for the home address and
e-mail, and a smaller one for the
phone number.

4 Run all punched shapes through a sticker machine.
To print the text directly to the shapes, use your
printed transparency as a guide and adhere the appro-
priate shapes over the text. Place the transparency
sheet with stickers back in your printer, and print again.
Remove the shapes from the transparency and adhere
to the front of the card.

5 Attach decorative brads as shown. If you want
a bit of additional decoration, apply stick-on
letters to add initials, a phrase, or sentiment to
the card.

sweet thirteen birthday coupons

designer: molly smith

Give her what she wants—what she really, really wants! When you tailor these cool coupons to the new teen's interests, you're always assured your gift will be a perfect fit.

materials

Heavyweight, two-sided decorative paper

Printer-compatible vellum

Glue stick or craft glue

Decorative fibers and ribbon

Tinted, self-sealing, translucent envelope, approximately 4½ x 5¾ inches (11.5 x 14.5 cm)

tools

Circle cutter

Scissors

Computer and printer

Hole punch

Perforating tool
Size: 3 inches
(7.6 cm) round

size:
card,
1½ x 1½ inches
(3.8 x 3.8 cm);
envelope,
3 x 3 ½ inches
(7.6 x 8.9 cm)

coupons

process

1 Cut seven, 3-inch (7.6 cm) circles from the double-sided decorative paper and set aside. Use your computer to generate text for a cover, a poem, and five gift coupons (see below). Center the text so it will fit within a 2-inch (5.1 cm) circle when printed. Print the text on printer-compatible vellum.

2 Using a 2½ -inch (5.5 cm) circle cutter, cut out the printed text for the cover and poem. Center each on two of the circles cut from decorative paper, then glue the vellum to the circles. Punch a hole in each circle, 1/4 inch (.6 cm) from the top.

3 Cut out the text for the five coupons using a 2½-inch (5.5 cm) circle cutter. Using a perforating tool, perforate straight across each circle slightly above the text. The perforations will allow the recipient to tear each coupon from the card. Pair a coupon circle with a decorative-paper circle. Line them up at their tops and punch a hole through both of them. Repeat pairing and punching the remaining vellum coupons and paper circles.

4 Gather several strands of coordinating fibers and ribbons. Thread them through the cover, poem, and pairs of coupons and decorative circles. Tie once using a simple overhand knot. For an added decorative touch, tie a narrow metallic ribbon around the stands at the top of the knot. Trim the ends of the ribbons at an angle, leaving various lengths from 2 to 3 inches (5.1 to 7.6 cm).

envelopes

Seal the translucent envelope. Make a new opening by trimming approximately 1½ inches (3.8 cm) off one of the sides. Cut a 1 x 4-inch (2.5 x 10 cm) strip from decorative paper. On the outside of the envelope, lay the strip flush with the edge of the opening and glue it in place to create a border.

Sayings

If you're at a loss for words, borrow these sayings for your coupon card. Otherwise, use them as inspiration when thinking of your own.

Cover Happy Birthday Sweet "13"

Poem *No longer a tween, you're a teen, it's true. So here are cool coupons just for you!*

Coupons *Friday Night Sleep Over (Invite some friends and have a party!) Day at the Spa (Facial, manicure, and pedicure with your best friend.) Lunch and a Movie (Your choice of restaurant and movie with friends.)Trip to the Mall (Shopping, more shopping, and fun!) Fun-to-Learn Class (Cooking, sewing, or scrapbooking-your choice.)*

come one, come all
circus invitation

Lions and tigers and bears—oh my! Since this project uses one-of-a kind vintage components, let the design act as an inspiration when gathering your own imagery and materials.

size:
Card without tickets,
2⅞ x 3⅜ inches
(7 x 6.1 cm);
mini-book,
1¼ x 1½ inch
(3.2 x 3.8 cm)

designers: linda and opie o'brien

materials

Vintage crayon box cover

Deconstructed tin can

Mini-eyelets

Gourd fragment

Ink

Wax crayons (optional)

Watercolor paper

Alphabet stamps and ink pad

Plastic and metal charms

Wood glue

Mini-brads

Double-sided tape

2 inches (5.1 cm)
of 20-gauge copper wire

Circus tickets

tools

Scissors

Craft knife

Tin shears

Pencil

Paper punch

Metal hole punch

Eyelet-setting tool

Wood burning tool

Mini-quilt iron (optional)

Decorative-edge deckle
scissors

Bone folder

Awl

Round-nose pliers

process

1 Using the scissors or craft knife, cut out your imagery for the front of the card. As shown, the clown image, which came from a vintage crayon box, measures $2\frac{7}{8}$ x $3\frac{3}{8}$ inches (7 x 6.1 cm). Use tin shears to cut a piece from a decon-structed tin can—the back of this card comes from a decorative animal-cracker tin. Trim the tin piece to the exact size as the front of the card.

2 Use a pencil to mark the placement of the holes, with one in each corner and two additional along the bottom. Make sure the holes are in the same position on the tin back as on the paper front. Punch holes in the paper using a paper punch and in the tin using a metal punch.

Line up the holes and use eyelets and the eyelet-setting tool to attach the front to the back. Since the tickets are inserted between the paper and tin, allow enough room between the top eyelets to accommodate the width of the tickets.

3 The cover of the book is made from a fragment of a hard-shell gourd that was cut with a craft knife to a 1¼- x 1½-inch (3.2 x 3.8 cm) piece. If using a gourd, use a wood-burning tool to create the borders and text. Color the cover with inks. The sides, as shown here, were finished with encaustic technique using wax crayons and a mini-quilt iron, but that is optional.

4 Cut a 1½- x 11-inch (3.8 x 27.9 cm) strip of watercolor paper. Use decorative-edge scissors to deckle the edges. Mark the paper at 1¼-inch (3.2 cm) intervals. Use a bone folder to score the lines, and then fold seven times using the accordion fold. Decorate each fold as desired, using paper or cloth images, mini-brads, and alphabet stamps to create words.

5 Attach one end of the folded paper to the cover. If you're using a gourd for the cover, adhere the paper using wood glue, and allow to dry. Attach the other end to the front side of the card using double-sided tape.

6 For the pull out clasp, use an awl to make a hole in the center of the right edge of the cover. Insert the copper wire in the hole, centering its length with half of it on the outside and half inside. On the inside of the cover, use round-nose pliers to shape the wire into a spiral. On the outside of the cover, string a charm on the wire before shaping the wire to a spiral. Bend both spirals to lie flush to the cover.

7 Attach the charms to the eyelet holes in the bottom of the card using star-shaped mini-brads. Insert the tickets, and your invitation is ready to go.

meandering fold-out book

designer: kim grant

Choosing just the right words for tiny greetings can be torture for those of us more accustomed to writing long sentiments. The multiple pages of this unique fold-out book provide ample space for flowing prose.

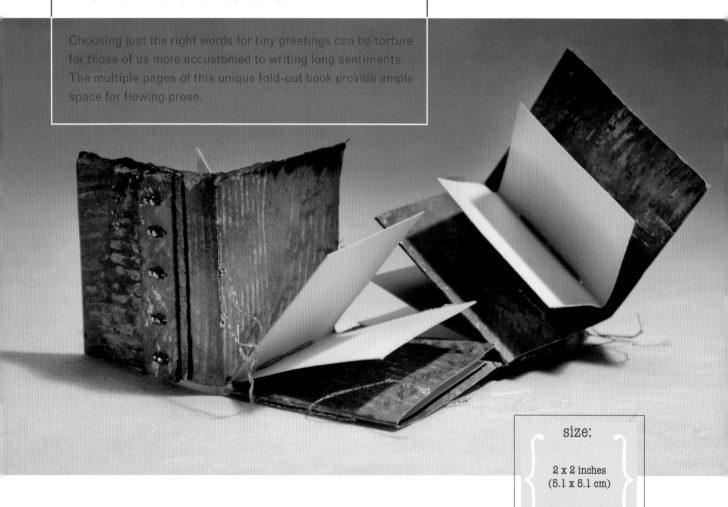

size:

{ 2 x 2 inches (5.1 x 5.1 cm) }

materials

Printmaking paper*

Acrylic paint

Metallic gold paint

Needle

Metallic gold embroidery floss

Gold seed beads

Embellishments of choice

Rubber stamps

Pens

tools

Flat brush, 1 inch (2.5 cm)
wide

Texture tools**

Metal ruler

Pencil

Scissors

Bone folder

*The designer chose printmaking paper for
its soft feel and smooth, sturdy surface,
which makes it easy to manipulate, paint,
and embellish.

**Can include purchased faux-painting texture
tools or those found around the house, such as
combs, forks, or bottle tops.

process

1 Cut a 6-inch (15.2 cm) square from printmaking
paper. Paint a base color of your choice on one
side. Before the paint dries,
use the texture tools of
choice to create shapes and
marks in the wet paint. Allow
to dry. Use the texture tools
to highlight the painted surface with metallic gold paint.
Allow to dry and repeat on
the other side of the paper.

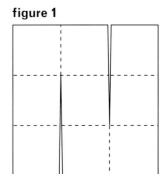

figure 1

2 Using a ruler and pen-
cil, divide the painted
paper into a grid of 2-inch
(5.1 cm) squares. As shown in
figure 1, cut one line 4 inches
(10.2 cm) into the grid, and
then turn the paper and cut
another 4-inch (10.2 cm) line.

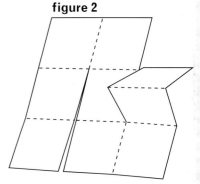

figure 2

3 Use a bone folder to
score all lines. As
shown in figure 2, start at
one corner of the paper and
accordion fold on the scored
lines. Keep folding over and
under, following the arrows,
as shown in figure 3. This
painted folded paper will

figure 3

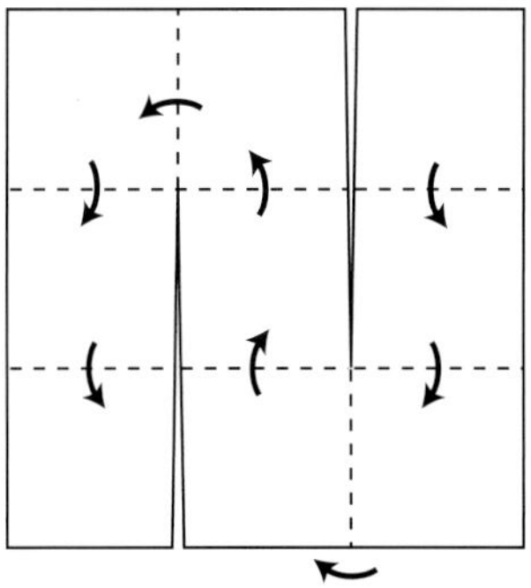

become the covers of the book. When you unfold it, you'll get a sense of where to attach the pages.

4 Here's where the creative fun begins. Cut windows into some sections, fold back corners, stitch on beads or scraps of papers. Embellish as desired until you feel the covers are complete—the objective is to create visual candy. There are no limits to the embellishments you can use. For example, try using eyelets, brads, copper or silver tape, wire, ribbons, charms, rusted washers, old nails, or small keys.

5 Count the number of folds in the book. For each fold cut a 1¾- x 3½-inch (4.4 x 8.9 cm) piece of printmaking paper, and then fold each in half. Note: For a softer feel, don't cut the paper with scissors; instead, tear it along the edges of a metal straightedge or deckle-edge tool.

6 With metallic embroidery floss, use the pamphlet stitch (see page 23) to attach the pages to the covers. Leave a long tail of thread after knotting off. This will add another texture to the book and will provide a length of thread for attaching beads if desired.

7 Decorate the interior pages with stitching and beading, rubber stamping, writing, drawing, and paper or fabric collage as desired.

8 To complete the book, make a closure for it from painted scrap paper. Measure around the folded book, adding 1 inch (2.5 cm) for overlap. Stitch the closure together, decorate with beads, and slip it over the book.

posey tic-tac-toe

Making these cards is as easy as picking posies in a garden. Layering vellum on simple prints is a great way to expand your visual palette.

designer: terry taylor

materials

Vellum in several colors

Decorative print paper

Commercially purchased cards
(or make your own)

Colorful brads

tools

Sticker machine

Scissors

Flower punches

process

1 Run small sheets of vellum through the sticker machine.

2 Cut the vellum into smaller portions and adhere them to the decorative print paper.

3 Punch floral shapes out of both the plain vellum and the print papers that are covered with vellum.

4 Cut narrow strips of vellum approximately the length and width of your card. Don't try to be precise—making the strips slightly irregular will increase visual interest.

5 Adhere the strips to the card in a grid.

6 Now, play tic-tac-toe and arrange the punched floral shapes on the cards as desired. Add brads to some of the flowers to add visual spice.

7 Decorate the envelopes as little or as much as you wish with other elements of choice.

size:

2 x 2½ inches
(5.1 x 6.4 cm)

sweet dreams sachet cards

Wish your favorite sleepyhead "sweet dreams" with
these collaged greetings. The miniscule sachets
tucked inside emanate the soothing scents of dried
rosemary and lavender.

materials

Card stock

Bottle cap

Acrylic paint

Paper remnants

Ephemera

Old photos

Decoupage medium

GlueSilk Scraps

Netting

Dried rosemary or lavender

Thread

Millinery flowers

tools

Scissors

Pencil

Straight edge

Bone folder

Hole punch

Disposable brush

Color photocopier

Sewing needle

process

1 From card stock, cut a card base that measures 4 x 2½ inches (10.2 x 6.4 cm). Mark the center line lightly with a pencil. Use a straight edge and bone folder to score and fold the card. Set aside.

2 Take a sheet of card stock. Dip the bottle cap into paint and use it to make circle impressions over the entire sheet. You can print all circles in one color, or use a smaller bottle cap to print different color circles over larger ones. Allow to dry

3 Use the hole punch to punch holes from interesting paper remnants. Sprinkle the dots about randomly on the card stock.

4 Cut out photos and/or ephemera to create a central collage image. Using a disposable brush with decoupage medium, adhere the collage and punched dots to the card stock.

5 On a color photocopier, reduce the collage to 25 percent. Cut out the small image and glue it to the front panel of the card base.

6 To make the small sachets, cut out 1-inch (2.5 cm) squares of silk and netting. Layer the squares with the netting on the outside and the silk on the inside. Place a small amount of dried rosemary or lavender in between the silk. Stitch closed through all layers. As a variation, sew small pouches, fill them with the herbs, and draw the top closed with a length of thread. Embellish the sachets with tiny millinery flowers.

designer: jean moore

materials

Card stock

Vintage paper doll images

Colored pencils or markers

Paper canvas

Decorative paper

White craft glue

Foam tape

Vintage letters (can be cut from old books) or tiny scrapbooking letters

1¼ -inch-high (3.2 cm) wooden spools in a variety of thread colors

tools

Computer, scanner, printer, or photocopier

Scissors

Craft knife

spoolie place cards

A friend of the designer coined the name "spoolies" after seeing these diminutive dollies. Use them as place cards for a little girl's birthday celebration. When the party's over, each guest can take her spoolie home.

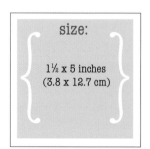

{ **size:**

1½ x 5 inches (3.8 x 12.7 cm) }

process

1 Scan or copy a paper doll and dress image—this one came from a 1937 children's activity book. You'll find a template for this little miss on page 124. Reduce or enlarge the image until the doll measures 1¼ x 3¼ inches (3.2 x 8.2 cm). Make sure to print or copy enough for all the spoolies you'll make. Use colored pencils or markers to color the images.

2 Cut a doll and dress image from the paper. At this point, don't worry about cutting them precisely around the outline.

3 Cut pieces of paper canvas and decorative paper that are a little larger than the width and height of the doll. Glue the doll image to one side of the paper canvas, and the decorative paper to the other side. Allow the layers to dry. The heavyweight paper canvas will enable the doll to stand.

4 Use the craft knife to carefully cut around the outline of the doll and through all layers of paper. Cut a small notch in the doll's right hand which will allow the doll to hold the banner.

5 As you did in step 3, layer and glue the dress image in the same way. When thoroughly dry, carefully cut around the image, leaving the white tabs on the dress if desired. Make sure to cut around the entire left arm on the dress image. This will enable you to loop the thread around the doll's wrist to hold the other end of the banner.

6 Use a small piece of foam tape to attach the dress to the paper doll. The tape helps to create a dimensional effect.

7 Cut out enough letters to spell the name. Glue the letters to card stock. When dry, cut the letters out, leaving a tab of card stock above each letter. The tabs, when folded, will enable the letters to hang from the thread.

8 Using the craft knife, cut a notch into and across the top of the spool. You want the doll's feet to slide into the notch, so make sure you cut it long enough. Put a dab of glue into the notch and slide the feet into place. Allow to dry.

9 Cut a generous length of thread from the spool being used for the place card. Tie a tiny loop on one end of the thread. Slip the loop over the doll's left wrist. Allow enough thread to drape across to the other arm.

10 Fold the tabs on the letters and put a dab of glue on each tab. Hang the letters on the thread by their tabs to spell out the name. Insert the end of the thread into the notch on the doll's right hand. Repeat for all dolls—and they're ready to party!

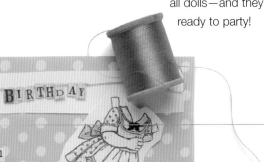

size:

{ 3 x 3 inches
(7.6 x 7.6 cm) }

materials

White, heavyweight, textured watercolor paper

Decoupage medium

White glitter

Double-sided tape

tools

Scissors

Bone folder

Craft knife

Ruler

Pencil

sparkling holiday pop-up

In shimmering white on white, heaven and nature sing and sparkle
for the holidays. Celebrate the winter season with this simple, elegant card.

process

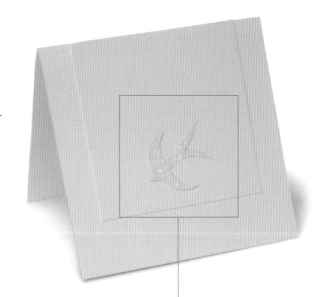

1 Cut a rectangle from the water-color paper measuring 3¼ x 6 inches (8.2 x 15.2 cm). Fold the paper in half. To prevent the paper from breaking at the fold, score the fold first using the bone folder or craft knife.

2 In order to make the tree pop-up, cut a tab inside the card. Following the directions for making a simple pop-up on page 24, measure and mark a spot 1½ inches (3.8 cm) down from the top of the card, and then measure down another ¼ inch (.6 cm) and make a second mark.

3 Using the marks as your guide, draw two parallel lines that extend ½ inch (1.3 cm) from either side of the center fold, making each line 1 inch long (2.5 cm). Use the craft knife to cut through the lines, and then fold the tab out at its center point.

4 To make the tree, use a piece of watercolor paper that is approximately 2¾ inches (7 cm) square. Fold it in half and draw a tree shape on one side. When you're satisfied with the shape, use your craft knife to cut out the trunk and branches. When you unfold it, you'll have a lovely tiny tree.

5 Brush decoupage medium on one side of the tree, and sprinkle it with glitter. Allow it to dry completely. Using double-sided tape, adhere the tree, glitter side out, to the tab.

6 To give the card its white-on-white layered look and to cover the cuts made for the tab on the outside of the card, take a piece of 2½ x 5-inch (6.5 x 12.7 cm) watercolor paper and fold it in half. Use double-sided tape to adhere this smaller card to the outside of the larger card.

7 Cut out a bird shape and coat it with glitter as you did for the tree. Adhere the bird to the front of the card using the decoupage medium as glue.

school days

Slide mounts are great to use. They provide you with instant mini-frames that you can collage, paint, distress, adorn, and embellish with all of your favorite things. Most of all—they're small!

size:

{ 2¼ x 2¼ inches
(5.6 x 5.6 cm) }

designer: chris schwartz

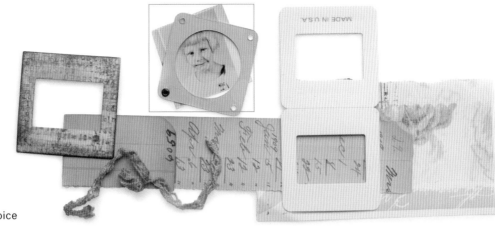

materials

Old school photos or images

Slide mounts

Decorative paper

Glue stick

Mica

Gold marker

Card stock

Embellishments of choice

tools

Computer, scanner, photo-editing software, printer, or photocopier

Craft knife

Ruler

Pencil

Bone folder

Metal ruler

Eyelet-setting tool (optional)

process

1 Scan several school photos of family and friends, reduce them to size, and print them in black and white. If you don't have a computer, use a photocopier to reduce and copy the images.

2 Cover the slide mounts in decorative papers of your choice. To insert the images, open the mount and apply glue to the inside surface. Place a piece of mica over the opening, and then glue the image behind the mica. Close the mount to seal. Use a gold marker to highlight the edges of the mount.

3 Cut a piece of card stock 2¼ x 9 inches (5.6 x 22.9 cm). Use a ruler and pencil to mark the strip at 2¼-inch (5.6 cm) intervals. Draw a line at each mark, and then use a bone folder to score all lines. Fold the strip using the accordion fold until you have a book that is 2¼ inches (5.6 cm) square.

4 Collage the panels of the book with decorative papers, old dictionary pages, assorted ephemera, and the slide mounts with pictures. Add pockets to some of the panels as desired—these are perfect for tucking in collaged tags and additional ephemera. You can even trim down a few slide mounts to fit into the pockets.

5 Continue to embellish the panels as desired with charms, watch faces, crystals, label holders, brads, eyelets, ribbon, buttons, or rubber stamps.

birthday fortunes
tag book

designer: jane reeves

Predict a wonderful year for your birthday boy or girl.
Controlling fortunes and imagery allow you to create a
thoughtful and humorous greeting.

size:

2⅜ x 4¾ inches
(5.2 x 12 cm)

materials

Fortunes from fortune cookies

Photos and images for collage

6 manila shipping tags

Decorative paper

Glue stick

Rubber stamps

Inks or acrylic paints

Various cords and strings

tools

Scissors

process

1 Select or collect five fortunes from fortune cookies and choose photos and other images to accompany each one. Copy and, if necessary, resize photos and images.

2 Collage the manila tags using the fortunes, images, photos, and decorative paper. Keep in mind that two open, facing tags will become a "spread." Design your collages accordingly to extend over both facing pages. Make sure you decorate a front and back cover.

3 Distress all of the tags using rubber stamps and acrylic paint or inks to achieve an antique look.

4 Stack the tags in order. Machine or hand stitch the tags together ½ inch (1.3 cm) from the straight edges. Cut a strip of decorative paper approximately 1½ x 2½ inches (3.8 x 6.4 cm), fold it lengthwise, and glue it to the end of the book to cover the stitching. Trim the decorative strip flush to the tags if necessary.

5 Tie strings and cording through the holes in all the tags.

6 Make a simple open-ended envelope from decorative paper, see the template on page 125. Distress the envelope to match the tags.

designer: luanne udell

collaged business cards

It's all about style. Whether your work is whimsical and colorful, quiet and serene, or stark and powerful, make sure your business cards reflect who you are.

size:
2 x 3 ½ inches
(5.1 x 8.9 cm);
2¾ x 3¼ inches
(7 x 8.2 cm);
2¾ x 4¾ inches
(5.6 x 12. 1cm);
3½ x 4 inches
(8.9 x 10.2 cm)

materials

Card stock

Decorative papers*

Collage elements**

Glue

Alphabet stamps or stickers (optional)

Marker pens

Rubber stamps, commercial
and hand-carved

tools

Scissors of craft knife

Ruler

Straight edge

Computer and printer

Decorative-edge scissors

*Used as shown: handmade papers, pages from
an old dictionary, old maps, cardboard, label
paper, and bark wrap.

**Including: junk metal, ribbon, raffia, vintage
postage stamps, handmade artifacts, name
labels, etc.

process

1 Measure and cut the card stock into standard
business-card-size 2- x 3½-inch (5.1 x8.9 cm)
rectangles, or into other non-standard sizes of
your choice.

2 Use the computer to generate the text for your contact information and print it on decorative papers.
Experiment with fonts to achieve different effects. Note:
If you have address labels or rubber stamps with this
information, you may want to use them on the cards.

You can also use alphabet stamps or
stickers, or cut letters and words out of
newspapers, magazines, or old books.
Handwritten words or phrases can also
be effective.

3 Now the fun begins—and you are limited only
by your imagination! Think about the elements
of your business—materials, techniques, or style—and
incorporate them into your cards. Use marker pens,
rubber stamps, and decorative-edge scissors to create
different effects. For example:

Materials Fiber artists can glue scraps, such as fabric,
yarn, felt, ribbon, etc, to the card; papermakers can use
swatches of their handmade paper; and painters can
make small samples of their work that they can attach to
the card.

Techniques Collage artists can use interesting stamps,
papers, and decorative elements to make tiny collages;
calligraphers can do a montage of letters or words; and
stamp carvers can carve and stamp original designs.

Style Capture the style of your business or art. On one
card, the designer used a piece of her polymer artifacts,
which she uses in her jewelry, and museum-style labeling.
Another card has a mini-fiber collage using dense stitching through many layers that reflects how the artist
makes her fiber art.

Tip Make these cards in batches rather than trying to
make one perfect card at a time. This allows you to
experiment with a variety of techniques and will create
cards that are unique yet coordinated.

treasure box

Transform a matchbox into a tiny treasure trove. Enclosing a book in the drawer allows you to deliver a hidden message beautifully.

designer: karen timm

materials

Decorative paper*

Double-sided tape

Paint (optional)

Ribbon or trim for book closure

Small snap (optional)

Thread or embroidery floss

16- and 18-gauge copper or brass wire

Beads or embellishments of choice

tools

Craft knife

Ruler or measuring tape

Scissors

Wire cutters

Round-nose pliers

Needle

Awl

*You can use any weight of paper to cover the outside of the matchbook, but use lightweight paper for covering the drawer.

size:

{ without drawer pull, 1½ x 2 inches (3.8 x 5.1cm) }

process

Covering the Slipcase

1 Measure around the outer slipcase of the matchbox. Cut a piece from the heavier weight decorative paper to size. You may wish to cut a piece from scrap paper first to act as a pattern.

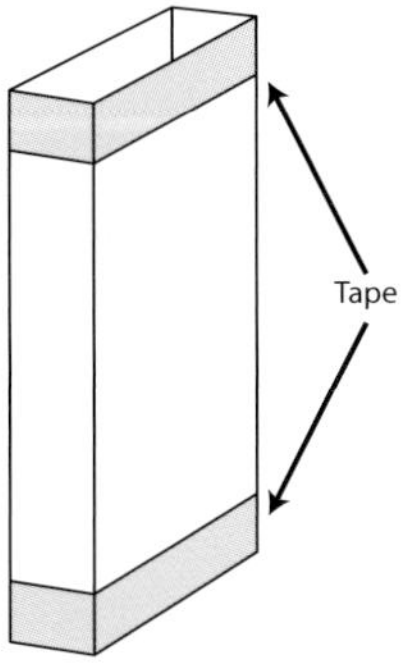

2 Apply double-sided tape around each end of the slipcase, as shown in figure 1, making sure the tape lies flush to the edges of the case.

figure 1

Tape

3 Wrap the paper around the slipcase. Begin by attaching the paper to one of the sides approximately ⅛ inch (.3 cm) from the corner. When you turn a corner, crease the paper lightly with your fingers to ensure that the paper will lie flat against the box.

4 Overlap your beginning point, bringing the paper flush to the edge of the last corner. Trim excess paper as needed.

Covering the Drawer

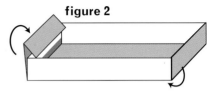

figure 2

1 Cut a strip of light-weight paper that will cover the drawer as shown in figure 2. Cut a little extra for an overlap.

Note: Make sure the paper is lightweight; otherwise the drawer will not slide easily in the slipcase.

2 Wrap the paper around the drawer as shown in figure 2. As you did when wrapping the slipcase, use your fingers to crease the paper at the corners for a flatter fit.

3 Carefully take off the folded paper. Apply double-sided tape around the drawer, wrapping the tape as you did for the paper. Apply two parallel strips to the outer edges of the drawer, making sure the tape lies flush with the edges.

4 If desired, paint the sides of the drawer that aren't covered with paper.

Wire Embellishments

1 Use the round-nose pliers to bend 16-gauge wire back and forth to create a freeform meandering design.

2 As you work, refer to the box to determine where you need to bend the wire to go around the corners. Slip the wire on and off the box throughout the bending process to make sure it will fit around your box. A snug fit is very important. Adjust the wire accordingly and trim any excess.

Tiny Book

1 Cut a cover for the book from decorative paper. Cut a strip that, when folded into three equal panels, will fit inside the drawer. Cut pages from any paper to fit inside the cover.

2 As shown in figure 3, fold the right-hand panel over the back panel, and the left-hand panel over that to become the cover. Open the folded paper and trim a bit off the edge of the right-hand panel to allow the book to lie flat in the matchbox.

figure 3

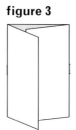

figure 4

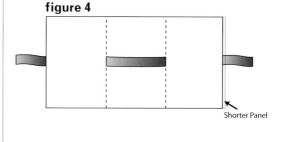

Shorter Panel

3 If desired, you can add a closure by cutting two small slits in the folds, and then thread them with ribbon or trim, as shown in figure 4. You can tie the closure or sew a little snap to it.

4 Slip the pages into the cover and use a needle and thread or embroidery floss to attach them using the pamphlet stitch (see page 23). Begin the stitch so the last knot is made on the inside, making sure the thread is fairly tight when tying the knot.

Drawer Handle

1 Use an awl to punch a small hole in the center top of the drawer.

2 Cut a small piece of 18-gauge wire, and use the round-nose pliers to make a circular "stop" on one end.

3 Thread the wire through the hole with the stop inside the drawer. Thread on beads or other embellishments as desired, and then use the pliers to make another stop at the end of the wire to hold the beads in place.

Variation You can make the decorated matchbox into a necklace. Simply attach beaded strands or decorative yarn or thread to both sides of the wire embellishment and finish as desired with a clasp of your choice.

artist trading card holder

Artist Trading Cards, or ATCs, are a popular way to share your art with others. The small cards are fun to make and collect. Here, designer Sharon Wisely has given them their own little home.

size:
Holder,
2½ x 3½ inches
(6.4 x 8.9 cm);
ATCs,
1½ x 2½ inches
(3.8 x 6.4 cm)

GM

CM

designer: sharon wisely

materials

Decorative paper

White acrylic paint

Sandpaper

Chipboard or
heavyweight
cardboard

Glue

Eyelets

Metallic gold marker

Pink vellum

Patterned acetate

Vintage photos or
images

Ephemera

Rubber stamps
and ink

Charms

Ribbon

tools

Paintbrush

Craft knife

Hole punch

Eyelet-setting tool

Sewing machine

process

1 Thin white acrylic paint with water and use it to whitewash a decorative patterned paper of choice. Allow to dry. Lightly distress the paper with sandpaper.

2 Glue the whitewashed paper to the chipboard. When dry, use the craft knife to cut two house shapes. You'll find a template on page 125.

3 Punch holes in the chipboard shapes, making sure the holes line up on the front and back cover. Use the eyelet-setting tool to set eyelets in the chipboard.

4 Use a metallic gold marker to edge the chipboard shapes. When dry, lightly sand the edges.

5 For the inside of the card, cut two house shapes from patterned paper. Cut pockets for the trading cards from vellum or patterned acetate. Using the sewing machine, stitch the pockets to the patterned shapes. Glue the stitched shapes to the inside of the chipboard shapes.

6 Create your own ATCs. Cut the card base from card stock to measure a scant 1½ x 2½ inches (3.8 x 6.4 cm). Have fun embellishing the cards with patterned papers, images, photos, ephemera, and rubber stamps. Add text, charms, and ribbons as desired. Tip: If the charms are too shiny, you may want to distress them with acrylic paint.

7 When the cards are finished, and all glue and paint are dry, slip the ATCs into their pockets. Tie the front and back of the holder together with ribbon.

crochet-motif greeting

designer: nikki-shell (nichola prested)

Many craft-savvy divas are accomplished in a wide range of techniques and have learned to mix and match them for fabulous results. If you're handy with a crochet hook (or knitting needle, or bead loom, or whatever!), why not use it when making cards.

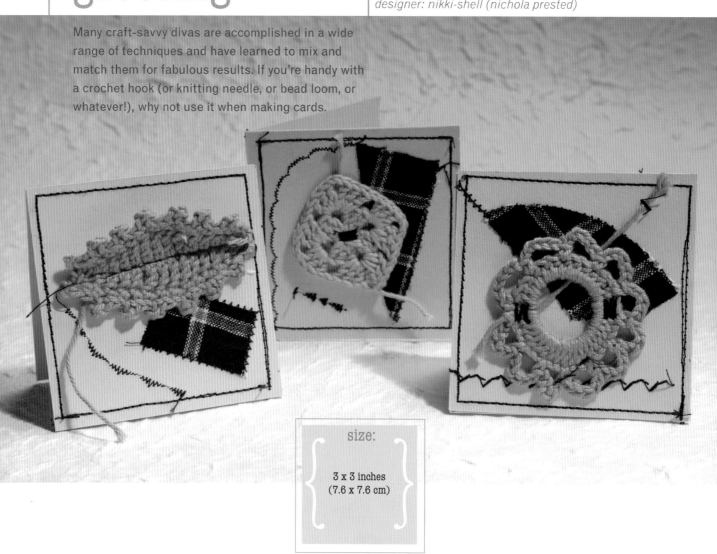

size:

{
3 x 3 inches
(7.6 x 7.6 cm)
}

materials

Yarn

Card stock

Ribbons, fabric scraps, and trim

Thread

tools

Crochet hook

Scissors

Ruler

Bone folder

Sewing machine

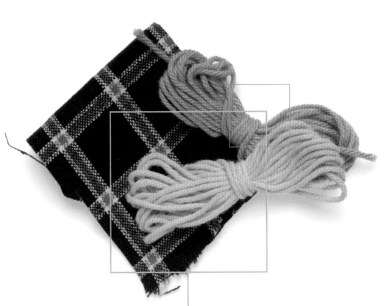

process

1 Crochet a small motif that will fit on the front of the card. You can find patterns for different shapes in crochet books or on the Internet. If you're a beginner, this is one way to practice and put your pieces to good use. If you're more accomplished, you can have loads of fun developing your own patterns. Leave the tails hanging from the motif.

2 Cut a piece of card stock 6 x 3 inches (15.2 x 7.6 cm) and fold it in half. Use a ruler and bone folder to score the paper before folding. Cut another piece of card stock 3 x 3 inches (7.6 x 7.6 cm) and set aside.

3 Arrange the ribbon, fabric scraps, and trim on the front panel. When you're satisfied with the place-ment, use the sewing machine to sew them to the card. If you want the card to have a more organic "raw" look, do not trim the threads after sewing. Position the cro-chet motif on top, and sew it in place.

4 Take the 3- x 3-inch (7.6 x7.6 cm) piece of card stock, place it on the inside cover, and use the sewing machine to sew around the edges. This hides the stitching from the front of the card and gives you more blank space for writing your message or greeting.

calligraphic
calling cards

Nothing makes an impression like an elegant calling card. Use Copperplate lettering and Majuscule forms as shown, or follow the technique using any lettering style you choose.

designer: mary teichman

size:

3½ x 2 inches
(8.9 x 5.1 cm)

rose card

materials

Masking tape

Ruled tracing paper
or drafting vellum

Watercolor paper, 140
lb

Erasable transfer
paper

Ink

Watercolors *

* Colors used as
shown: alizarin
crimson; cadmium
yellow; Winsor green;
burnt umber; and black

tools

#2 pencil

Drafting Table

Photocopier (optional)

Ruler

Craft knife

T-square

Calligraphy pen

Small sable watercolor brushes

Kneaded eraser

Computer, scanner,
publishing software, printer
(optional)

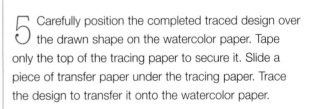

process

1 Begin by looking on the Internet or in calligraphy
books for sample styles of Copperplate lettering.
Make a template for the card by taping a piece of tracing paper to your drafting table and drawing the shape
of the calling card on it. Use another piece of tracing
paper and a pencil to experiment with the Copperplate
letter forms needed for the monogram.

2 When satisfied, measure the length of the monogram, find the center, and trace it onto the template. If you've made the monogram too large, use a
photocopier to reduce its size before tracing.

3 Find a reference illustration for the card. Trace the
illustration, reducing it if necessary. Carefully position it under the
monogram, and
then trace it onto
the template.

4 Cut a small
piece of watercol-
or paper slightly larger
than the card. Using a
T-square, line the paper up
with the edge of the table.
Use masking tape to hold it
in place. Using a ruler and
T-Square, measure and
draw the shape of the calling
card onto the
watercolor paper.

5 Carefully position the completed traced design over
the drawn shape on the watercolor paper. Tape
only the top of the tracing paper to secure it. Slide a
piece of transfer paper under the tracing paper. Trace
the design to transfer it onto the watercolor paper.

6 Practice using your calligraphy pen and ink on a
scrap of the watercolor paper before writing on the
finished card. If you aren't a calligrapher, use a very fine
watercolor brush or fine-point ink pen to trace the letters. Scribe the monogram on the card and allow the
ink to dry. Use the small brushes and watercolors to
paint the motif.

7 Carefully cut the borders of the card using the craft knife and a T-square. Erase any visible guide lines with the kneaded eraser.

8 For the reverse side, use ruled tracing paper to determine your design for the lettering until satisfied. If needed, reduce it on a photocopier to fit. As you did for the front of the card, transfer the name to the back, ink the monogram, allow to dry, and erase any visible lines.

Tip If you need only a few cards, make each by hand. If you need multiple copies, scan the design into your computer, use a publishing program to size, and then print it out. You can also use a color photocopier to reproduce the image.

gold leaf card

materials

Blue raised-ridge paper

22-karat gold leaf

Adhesive ink for application of gold leaf

Ink

tools

Soft brush

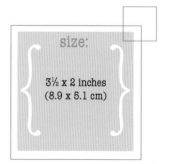

size:

3½ x 2 inches
(8.9 x 5.1 cm)

process

1 Choose your lettering style. This card uses Majuscule (capital) lettering forms based on an old Roman script from the sixteenth century.

2 As you did in steps 1 and 2 for the Rose Card, trace your monogram on the template. Following steps 4 and 5 for the Rose Card, transfer your design to the paper.

3 To apply the gold leaf, use adhesive ink to scribe the monogram as you would using calligraphy ink. Let the adhesive dry. Cut a sheet of gold leaf in half. Keeping your hands steady, apply the leaf to the mono-

gram. Press hard with your thumb, being careful not to scrape the gold with your nail. Remove the leaf that did not adhere, and then use a soft brush to remove any excess gold. If you missed some spots, reapply the adhesive to those spots and repeat the application. Erase any visible guidelines.

4 Trim the edges of the card, turn it over, scribe the back with the name using adhesive ink, and apply the gold leaf as in step 3.

Tip To retain the dazzling effect of the gold leaf, reproduce this card by hand. The beauty and luster of the gold leaf will be lost in the scanning or photocopying process.

seasonal
stamped place cards

designer: susan mcbride

Stamps, whether hand-carved or store-bought, are a great tool for making quick multiple designs. Here's an example of seasonal dining cards made by stamping textured papers.

materials

Heavyweight textured paper

Ink pads or acrylic paint and brayer

Tissue or mulberry paper in a variety of colors

Stamps, hand-carved or store-bought

Double-sided tape

Decoupage medium

Glitter (optional)

Pen and ink

Stands or holders for the cards

tools

Scissors

Craft knife

{ size:

2 x 2½ inches
(5.1 x 6.4 cm) }

process

1 Cut the heavyweight textured paper into 2- x 2½-inch (5.1 x 6.4 cm) rectangles.

2 Ink the stamps in colors you like and press them onto tissue or mulberry paper. Allow to dry completely.

3 Carefully cut out the stamped shapes and adhere them to the textured-paper rectangles using either double-sided tape or decoupage medium. If you wish, add some glitter by painting on a small amount of decoupage medium, and then sprinkling glitter on top.

4 To add interest and get the most from the textured papers, cut out leaves orshapes from the tissue or mulberry paper and add them to your designs by pasting them in place. This gives dimension and color to the graphic stamp design.

5 Brayer painting is also a nice way to show off the texture of a paper. Simply apply paint or ink to the textured paper with a brayer. Allow to dry before cutting into a desired shape.

6 Once the cards are dry, write your friends' names on them, place them on decorative stands or holders—and go get dressed!

mini-garland
greetings

Adorn your cards or packages with garland greetings.
Better yet, use them anytime you want to deliver a
surprise message-simply string them where they're
sure to be found.

designer: hope wallace

size:

{ triangles
1 x 1¾ inches
(2.5 x 4.4 cm);
length
36 inches (.9m) }

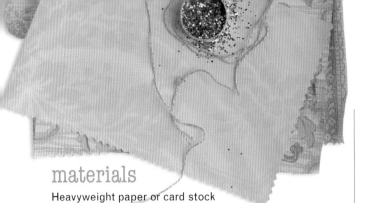

materials

Heavyweight paper or card stock

Vintage paper or wallpaper

Decoupage medium

Glue

Cord or raffia

tools

Triangle punch

Scissors

Glue brush

process

1 Using the triangle punch or scissors, make several triangles from heavyweight paper or card stock.

2 Decorate the triangles with vintage papers or wallpapers. Adhere the paper to the triangles using a brush and decoupage medium.

3 Adhere vintage letters or words to each banner. Allow the decorated triangles to dry. Tip: Vintage spelling books are a good source for finding text in old-fashioned fonts.

4 Lay the triangles on your work surface, spacing them as desired for your garland. Use glue to attach the cord or raffia to the triangles.

Variation Use a circle punch to make your shapes. Adhere vintage paper and letters as you did for the triangles. Apply glitter to the edges. Use an eyelet-setting tool to affix an eyelet at the top of each circle. Slip the circles on a metallic cord, using a simple overhand knot to secure each in place as you string them.

oh baby!

designer: molly smith

What's cuter than a tiny baby? Tiny cards, of course!
Use these to announce a birth or enclose them in a
gift. They're sure to trigger an admiring response.

materials

Blue and pink textured card stock

Clear, printer-compatible vellum

White craft glue

Satin ribbon, ⅛ inch (.3 cm) wide

1-inch mini clothespins

10 to 20, 2mm pearls

Craft chalk and applicator

Tiny baby sticker

Alphabet stamps or stickers
(optional)

tools

Diamond- and
heart-shaped
border punches

Paper trimmer

Computer and printer

Scoring tool

Deckle-edge ruler

Scissors

Hot glue gun and glue sticks

> size:
>
> 1¾ x 1 inches
> (3.2 x 2.5 cm)

Baby Girl Card

process

1 Punch a border on the pink textured card stock using the heart punch. Trim the paper to measure 2¼ x 1 inch (5.6 x 2.5 cm). Score the card 1 inch (2.5 cm) from the unpunched edge and fold. The punched border will extend from the edge of the card on the front panel.

2 Using a computer, center the text to cover an area approximately 1 inch (2.5 cm) square when printed. Print the text on printer-friendly vellum. If you wish to use alphabet stamps or stickers, make sure to use a font that is approximately ⅝ inches (1.6 cm) tall.

3 Using the deckle-edge ruler, tear around the edges of the printed vellum to make a ¾- x 1-inch (1.9 x 2.5 cm) overlay. Glue the vellum to the card, lining it up on the right at the base of the punched design.

4 Make a tiny bow from a 6-inch (15.2 cm) length of pink ribbon. Trim the ends of the bow on the diagonal. Using hot glue, adhere the bow to a clothespin. String a dozen 2mm white pearls on white string. Tie the ends in a double knot, trimming the string to leave a ½-inch (1.5 cm) tail. Attach the ring of pearls by clipping it to the front of the card with the tiny clothespin.

5 You'll find an envelope pattern on page124. Make it from white card stock, and once it's folded and glued, use craft chalk to lightly highlight its edges and seam.

Baby Boy Card

Punch a piece of blue textured card stock with a decorative diamond border punch. Follow directions above to complete the card. In lieu of pearls, apply a baby sticker to the front of the card. Make a bow using a length of blue satin ribbon. Tie a single knot and trim ends at an angle. Adhere to the clothespin using a glue gun. Clip the clothespin to the top of the card as shown. Make an envelope using the pattern on page 124, highlighting the edges and seam with chalk.

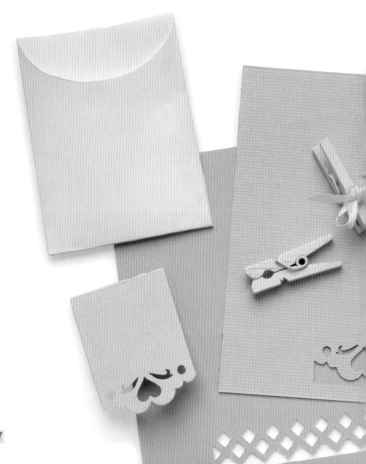

stacked deck

Solitaire will never be the same. Trick this altered deck
with visual punch and you'll always come up aces.

designer: jen swearington

materials

Images for collage

Paint, inks, decorative pens

Playing cards

Alphabet stamps (optional)

Decoupage medium or glue

Thread

Embellishments of choice

tools

Scissors

Sewing machines

process

1 Gather materials for collage, using vintage images and text.

2 Use paint, inks, or decorative pens to create a background on the face of the playing card.

3 Use decoupage medium or glue to adhere images. Create text using alphabet stamps or cut vintage text from old books or other sources and adhere.

4 Run the card through the sewing machine. Use decorative stitching if desired, follow a pattern, or let your stitches wander. Apply trim to some of the cards.

Tip Wondering how to use your decorated deck? Here are a few ideas.

✳ Tailor a greeting and send it to your favorite King or Queen of Hearts—or mischievous knave.

✳ Send a message to a poker-playing pal or bantering bridge partner.

✳ Stack the deck with sayings of prodigious prognostication, and use it to tell fortunes.

---

nested cards

It's fun to get a card within a card. For this project, multiply that by six. As with nesting dolls, the enjoyment intensifies with the opening of each successively smaller envelope.

designer: luanne udell

size:
Cards,
largest to smallest,
4 x 4 inches
(10.2 x 10.2 cm);
3½ x 3½ inches
(8.9 x 8.9 cm);
2¾ x 2¾ inches
(7 x 7 cm);
2¼ x 2¼ inches
(5.7 x 5.7 cm);
1½ x 1½ inches
(3.8 x 3.8 cm);
¾ x ¾ inch
(1.9 x 1.9 cm)

materials

Craft paper

Card stock, light brown on one side, dark brown on the other

Decorative elements of your choice

Glue

tools

Mat knife

See-through ruler

Bone folder

Scissors

Computer and printer (optional)

envelopes

process

1 Using the mat knife, cut six squares from craft paper measuring 7, 6, 5, 4, 3, and 2 inches (17.8, 15.2, 12.7, 10.2, 7.6, 5.1 cm). Using a see-through ruler to measure and a bone folder to score and fold, make six square envelopes following the template on page 125. Use scissors to clip small triangles from the center of each side of the square. Fold the side flaps in first and glue. Then fold the bottom flap up and glue to the side flaps. (See Handmade Envelopes on page 14.)

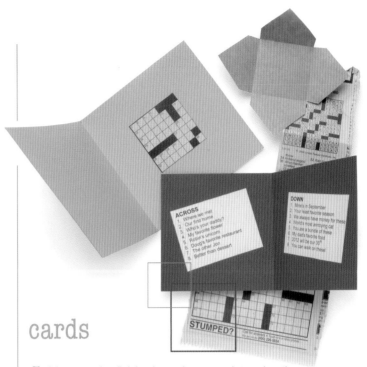

cards

1 Measure the finished envelopes to determine the size of each card. A finished card needs to be 1/8 to 3/8 inch (.3 to 1 cm) smaller than the envelope. Cut the card stock accordingly and fold it. Remember, in order to make a square card, start with a rectangle. For example, to make a card that is 4 inches (10.2 cm) square, you need to cut a 4- x 8-inch (10.2 x 20.3 cm) rectangle that you will fold in half.

2 Use your computer to generate text for your cards. You can also use alphabet stamps and stickers. Decorate the cover of each card to create a sequential message. Continue to decorate the cards as desired. As shown, crossword puzzles and text cut from newspapers finished this design.

3 Place each card in its envelope, nesting each inside the other, smallest to largest.

buttoned-up gift tags

designer: hope wallace

Sometimes the littlest details make the difference. Pearly, loop-backed buttons not only accent these tags, they provide a way to attach the colorful string.

materials

Card stock

Decorative paper in vintage designs Vintage text or letters

Decoupage medium

Glue

Embellishments of choice

Loop-backed buttons

Decorative string

tools

Shaped punches

Decorative-edge scissors (optional)

Scissors

Glue brush

Awl

Hot glue gun and glue sticks

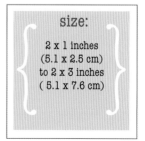

{ **size:**

2 x 1 inches
(5.1 x 2.5 cm)
to 2 x 3 inches
(5.1 x 7.6 cm) }

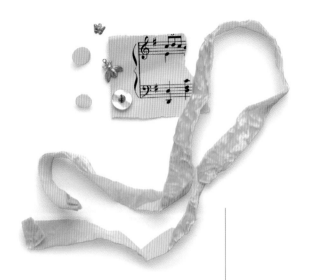

process

1 Use the shaped punches to make shapes of your choice from card stock. For variety, use decorative-edge scissors to cut out some of the shapes.

2 Apply vintage paper to the shapes using decoupage medium. Adhere words or letters to the cards with decoupage medium or glue.

3 Have fun embellishing the shapes. Add ribbons or charms, apply glitter around the edges, or attach a flirty crepe-paper ruffle.

4 Use an awl to pierce a small hole in the card where you plan to attach the button. Insert the loop of the button into the hole. Use a little dab of hot glue to secure the button to the front of the card.

5 Using a simple knot, tie a length of string to the button loop, leaving two ends free to use when attaching the tag to your gift.

quotation bookmarks

Celebrate the joy of reading with bookmark cards. They make a perfect greeting for all the booklovers in your life.

designer: jane reeves

size:
Small,
1½ x 5 inches
(3.8 x12.7 cm);
large,
2¼ x 7 inches
(5.7 x 17.8 cm)

materials

Card stock

Collage images

Quotations about books and reading

Colored pencils (optional)

Acrylic paint or ink

Decorative paper

Glue stick

Round tags with metal edges

Ribbon, string, or cording

tools

Scissors

Hole punch

Photocopier

process

1 Using the templates on page 125 as your guide, cut out bookmark shapes from card stock. Punch holes at either end of each bookmark as shown on the template.

2 Use a photocopier to copy collage images and quotes of your choice. Color them with colored pencils if desired, and distress them with paint or ink to give them an antiqued look. Note: You can generate the quotes and the names of the authors on your computer. Just make sure the printed text will fit on the tag once you cut it out.

3 Create small collages on the bookmarks by gluing the images and decorative paper to the front and back of card. Glue the quotation on the front of the tag and the author's name on the back.

4 Using ribbon, string, or cording, tie the tag to the bookmark, adding a tassel at the top.

creative
calling cards

Using vintage materials hand-in-hand with the latest products and technology can produce interesting retro results. The designer created an array of calling cards that shows off her range of talents.

designer: jane powell

duplicate jane

materials

Soft carving block or large eraser

Black ink

White paper

Card stock

tools

Small motorized craft tool or carving tools

Computer, scanner, photo-editing software, printer

process

Carve an image into a soft-carving block or large eraser. Stamp it with black ink on white paper, and then scan the image into the computer. Using photo-editing software, duplicate the image multiple times, leaving a text block for your name and e-mail address. Print the image, and then copy it onto colored card stock.

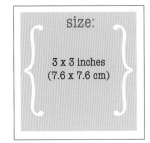

rust book

materials

Purchased mini-book

Acrylic matte medium

Paint-on iron and rust finishes

Copper coating

Patina finishes

Ink-jet transfer paper

Button

Glue

Decorative fiber

Beads or embellishments of choice

tools

Paintbrush

Computer, scanner, printer

process

Open the book at its middle. Using the matte medium, seal the edges of the pages together. Glue the cooresponding page block to either the front or back cover. Apply the rust finish over the iron finish and allow to dry. Add copper coating and green and blue patinas to complete the effect. Apply an ink-jet transfer image and name and address to the open pages. Adhere a vintage button to the front. Embellish the book with decorative fiber and beads as desired.

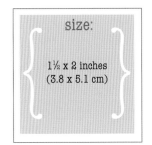

house slide

materials

Slide mount

Paint-on iron and rust finishes

Old file divider

Walnut ink

Ink-jet transfer paper

Transparency sheet Glue

Ribbon

tools

Paintbrush

Scissors

Computer, photo-editing software, printer

Hole punch

process

Apply the iron finish then the rust to the slide mount. Cut out a house shape from an old manila file divider and distress it with walnut ink. Generate computer images and print them on transfer paper. Transfer the images to the distressed shape. Generate the text for the name and address, and print it on a transparency sheet. Adhere the printed transparency to the slide, and then adhere the slide to the distressed shape. Trim as needed. Punch a hole at the top and attach the ribbon.

metal box

materials

Small metal box

Word stamps

Ink

Shrink plastic

Wire

Metal shapes

Vintage papers

Decoupage medium

tools

Awl

Wire cutters

Pliers

Paintbrush

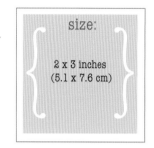

process

If needed, remove the painted finished from the box, and then stamp it with a random word stamp using black ink. Use an awl to punch holes in the sides of the box. Use wire to attach shrink-plastic hands or charms. Adhere a metal shape to the top, and glue a shrink-plastic face onto the shape. Collage the inside of the box using decoupage medium with vintage papers, including text with your name and town.

red adressograph

materials

Vintage address card*
Red acrylic paint
Old ledger paper
Acrylic matte medium

tools

Paintbrush
Computer, printer

*A precursor to our circular desktop files

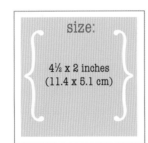

size:

4½ x 2 inches
(11.4 x 5.1 cm)

process

Paint the card. Generate text in the computer using a typewriter font, and print it on old ledger paper. Adhere the ledger paper to the card, and apply acrylic matte medium over the printed paper only.

yarn tied
vintage textile punch card

materials

Vintage textile card*
Decorative fibers
Ribbons
Threads
Old ledger paper
Acrylic matte medium
Card stock

tools

Computer, printer
Paintbrush

*A card with punched holes

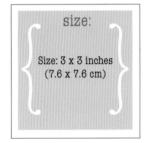

jane powell
random arts
Saluda • North Carolina

size:

Size: 3 x 3 inches
(7.6 x 7.6 cm)

process

If you can't find a vintage textile card, punch holes in a piece of fiberboard and distress as desired. Weave random fibers, ribbons, and threads through the holes. Generate text in a computer and adhere to the card using matte medium. Cover the back with a piece of card stock.

origami with heart

It's easy to give your heart away with this clever little card. A simple origami fold creates all the ins and outs you need to multiply your loving sentiment. Think they'll get the message?

materials

Handmade paper

Mat board

White craft glue

Waxed linen thread
or embroidery floss

tools

Craft knife

Awl

Embroidery
needle

size:

3 x 3 inches
(7.6 x 7.6 cm)

designer: claudia lee

process

1 Start with a 6-inch (15.2 cm) square of handmade paper in a color of your choice. Fold it as shown in figure 1. Open the paper, and following figure 2, fold two folds—one vertical, one horizontal.

2 Using the creases from the folds as your guidelines, bring point x to point o, folding in the sides, as shown in figure 3. When finished, you will have a 3-inch (7.6 cm) square.

3 Cut a 2-inch (5.1cm) square from mat board to use as a template for the window. Open the folded paper. Notice that two of the squares do not have diagonal centerfolds. Center the template on one of the squares without a centerfold, and cut around the template using the craft knife.

4 Cut a heart shape from the 2-inch square you used for your window template. Make sure the heart will fit in the window and adjust as needed. Lay the heart template on paper in a color of your choice. Use the craft knife to cut out two hearts.

5 Fold the hearts in half. With the card open, place the folds of the hearts on the centerfolds of the two squares. Make sure you line up the hearts on the fold lines, which will make them look like one heart when the card is closed. Glue the hearts in place.

6 Trim the heart template to make a slightly smaller heart shape, and then use it to make two more hearts in a color or your choice. Position them over the two larger hearts, and glue them in place.

7 Cut a 2½-inch (7 cm) square from handmade paper. Stitch a decorative border around its edge, center it, and glue it to the inside back panel of the card.

figure 1

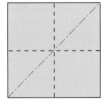

figure 2

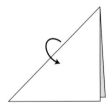
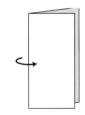

figure 3

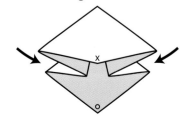

artful swivel card

A simple cut and fold enables the center panel of this card to swing out when opened. It's a perfect design when you want to highlight a special image or sentiment.

size:
2 x 2 ¾ inches
(5.1 x 7 cm);
2½ x 3½ inches
(6.4 x 8.9 cm)

designer: chris schwartz

materials

Tracing paper

Card stock

Decorative papers

Stamps and ink pad

Images

Embellishments
of choice

Glue

Copper foil

Brads

Ribbon

Eyelets

tools

Pencil

Craft knife

Straightedge

Bone folder

Eyelet-setting tool

process

1 Trace the template on page 125. You may reduce or enlarge the template to your desired dimensions. Transfer the tracing to card stock and cut it out.

2 Use the craft knife to cut around the center rectangle as indicated on the template. Use the straightedge and bone folder to score and fold the lines above and below it.

3 Enjoy decorating the card—stamp, paint, embellish as desired. Since both sides of the card will be visible when opened, make sure you finish both the front and back of the card.

4 Cut shapes from copper foil. Attach the foil and artful stamped images to the center panel using eyelets and an eyelet setting tool. Attach ribbons if desired.

sweetheart card

Unwrapping this card is just half the fun—from the organza bag to the tiny drawer with its secret beaded message. The other half is knowing someone out there loves you.

designer: anne igou

size:

{ 3 x 3 inches
(7.6 x 7.6 cm) }

materials

Polymer clay, one block each
in black and raspberry

Rubber stamps

Iridescent highlighting powder

Flat-back crystals

Matchbox

Acrylic paint,
red and silver pearl

Card stock

Embossing foil

Polymer bonding glue

Gold foil

Alphabet stamps

6 gold head pins

24-gauge gold wire

Seed beads

4mm clear bicone crystals

Eyelets

Ribbon

Small organza bag

tools

Polymer tools

Heart-shaped cutter

Scissors

Paintbrush

Scissors

Heat gun

Piercing tool

Round-nose pliers

Wire cutters

Craft knife

process

1 Condition the black clay, flatten it, and use a rubber stamp to impress a texture. Use your fingers to carefully apply iridescent highlighting powder to the raised surfaces. Use a heart-shaped cutter to cut out the heart. Press small, red, flat-back crystals into the clay until secure. Cut the heart into two sections. Carefully set aside.

2 Roll eight tiny balls from the raspberry clay and shape by hand into hearts. Make a slightly larger heart from the same color, and press a red crystal into its center. Use black clay to make three hearts for the bag, pressing a red, flat-back crystal into the center of each. Set aside.

3 Take the matchbox, remove the drawer, and paint all sides with red acrylic paint. Allow to dry. Make the card, following the template on page 124.

4 For the box cover, condition the black clay, flatten it, and then rubber stamp it with an overall script pattern. Apply a small piece of the embossing foil to the stamped surface. Use a light, even pressure with

your fingertips to burnish (rub) the foil into the clay. To complete the embossing, use a heat gun over the foil to flash set it. Remove the backing, leaving the foil stuck to the clay.

5 Apply the silver pearl acrylic paint to the clay sheet, making sure all recessed areas are covered. Use a rag to remove all paint from the raised foil-embossed areas, leaving paint in the recessed script only.

6 Use polymer glue to adhere the clay sheet around the matchbox slipcase, trimming any excess clay. From the gold foil, cut a heart shape that will fit on the cover of the box, and adhere it using the polymer glue. Adhere the larger raspberry-colored heart made in step 2 to the foil heart.

7 Make the beads for the inside of the matchbox by rolling small balls of black clay, flattening them

slightly, and then pressing a letter stamp into each one until you have enough letters for your secret message. Pierce each bead with a piercing tool and apply silver pearl paint as you did in step 4 to highlight the recessed letters only.

8 Following the manufacturer's instructions, bake all clay pieces and allow to cool completely.

9 Poke three holes at equal distances in the top of the matchbox. Using round-nose pliers and wire cutters, fashion the head pins, wire, seed beads, bicone crystals, and alphabet beads into the word dangles for inside the box. Attach the dangles through the punched holes.

10 Adhere the matchbox to the inside back panel of the card. Glue the heart halves to the front of the card, and the small hearts to the cover and the back inside panel. Glue the black hearts to the organza bag. For the closure, use the craft knife to poke two holes through the heart halves and card stock. Use polymer glue to set eyelets in the holes, and use a ribbon for the tie closure.

hidden-hello
puzzle greeting

designer: margert kruljac

It's no puzzle—everyone loves a secret. Send this little charmer when you want to keep your message strictly hush-hush.

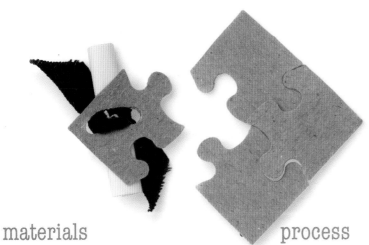

materials

Thin cardboard

Decorative paper

Glue

Stick-on acrylic letters

Plain paper

Printed twill tape

tools

Puzzle punch

Awl

Small hole punch

process

1 Use the puzzle punch to punch four pieces each from thin cardboard and decorative paper. Adhere the decorative paper pieces to the cardboard.

2 Adhere the acrylic letters to one of the pieces.

3 Use an awl or tiny hole punch to make two small holes, approximately ¼ inch (.6 cm) apart, in the puzzle piece that will lie opposite the piece with the letters.

4 Write a message on a small piece of plain paper and roll it up. Thread the printed twill through the holes, and tie the twill around the rolled message to hold it in place.

5 Make a small envelope from decorative paper to hold the puzzle pieces. You'll find a template on page 125.

mosaic
calling cards

designer: kim grant

Complex. Colorful. Bright. Bold. Do these words describe you? If so, why settle for the humdrum? Announce yourself to the world with these unique calling cards.

materials

Watercolor paper

Muslin

Thread

Rubber stamps

Acrylic paint

Metallic gold paint

tools

Craft knife

Scissors

Sewing needle

Sewing machine (optional)

Hot glue gun and glue sticks

1-inch (2.5 cm) flat brush

size:

{ 3 x 2 inches
(7.6 x 5.1 cm) }

process

1 Use the craft knife to cut out a 3- x 2-inch (7.6 x 5.1 cm) piece of watercolor paper for your card base. Cut a piece the same size from muslin. Hand or machine stitch around the edge of the card.

2 Rubber stamp your name on the muslin. Then sew the fabric to the back of the card.

3 Cut out six, 1-inch (2.5 cm) squares from the watercolor paper. Use the hot glue to draw shapes or designs on each one. Allow to cool.

4 Use the acrylic paint to paint each square a different color. Try unique color combinations. Using complementary colors will create a bright, inviting card. Allow to dry. Use metallic gold paint to highlight the raised designs made by the hot glue.

5 Use hot glue to adhere the painted-paper squares to the card base. Apply the glue directly to the base. If you apply the hot glue to the back of the paper squares, the heat from the glue gun will melt your painted designs. Allow to dry.

oh-sew-sweet stitched cards

Simple stitching adds so much to these sweet little cards. The extra pages you add, using the easy pamphlet stitch, allow you to truly extend your greetings.

designer: claudia lee

materials

Heavyweight paper

Text-weight paper for insert

Waxed linen thread
or embroidery floss

Glue

tools

Scissors

Embroidery needle

Awl

process

1 Start with a piece of heavyweight paper measuring 2½ x 5 inches (6.4 x 12.7 cm). Cut a piece of text-weight paper to measure 2¼ x 4¾ inches (5.6 x 12.1 cm).

2 Fold both papers in half, and insert the text-weight paper into the heavier weight card. Use the pamphlet stitch (see page 23) to sew the pages into the cover.

3 Cut out the shapes or designs you wish to put on the cover of your card. Before stitching, lay the shapes on foam core or corrugated cardboard and use an awl to pierce the stitching holes. Complete the stitching, using needle and thread.

4 Glue the stitched panel to the front of the card. If desired, adhere embellishments of you choice, such as the small dragonfly shown here.

5 You'll find a template for the envelope on page 124. Before gluing it together, you may want to add stitching to the envelope's back panel. As you did in step 3, stitch the shapes as desired and then glue them on. You can add a few decorative stitches at the corners if desired. To hide the stitching on the inside back panel of the envelope, cut a square to fit the back panel, and then glue it to the inside before assembling the envelope.

treasured sweetness

This card-within-a-card has a pop-up at its center. Use images from a vintage landscape postcard to create a nostalgic background for the cover collage.

materials

Vintage photos and postcards

Rubber stamp or alphabet stamps

Gold marker

Glue stick

Decorative paper with script pattern

Acrylic paint, Titan-buff

Card stock

Decoupage medium

Double-sided tape

Vintage button cards

Clear, round acrylic bauble

Embellishments of choice

size:

{ 3 x 3¾ inches (7.6 x 9.5 cm) }

tools

Computer, scanner, printer or photocopier

Scissors

1-inch (2.5 cm) disposable paint brush

Pencil

Ruler

Craft knife

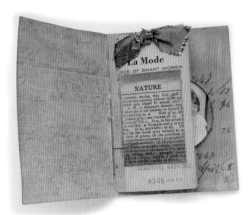 

process

1 Select favorite old photos or a landscape postcard to make a simple collaged background. If you have a computer and scanner, scan and reduce your images to size. If you don't have a computer, use a color photocopier to copy and reduce images as needed. Incorporate text into the collage if desired, using a rubber stamp with a phrase or alphabet stamps to create your own.

2 With a light touch to achieve a spatter effect, use the gold marker to texture the landscape background with highlights. Adhere a cut-out image (as shown here, the little girl) to the foreground of the collage.

3 Take the decorative paper with the script pattern and antique it by dry-brushing it using a disposable brush with the Titan-buff acrylic paint. Allow to dry.

4 Fold a piece of card stock in half for your card base. Adhere the antiqued paper to the card stock with decoupage medium. Allow to dry, and then glue the collage to the front of the card.

5 Use double-sided tape to attach two vintage button cards together. Then use the tape to attach them to the inside of the card base, making a card-within-a-card.

6 Make the pop-up by first folding a 1- x 4-inch (2.5 x 10.2 cm) strip of card stock in half. Following the directions for making a simple pop-up on page 24, mark two parallel lines on the strip, use a craft knife to cut the lines, and then fold the tab out. Adhere the strip at the center of the opened card. Glue an image onto the clear bauble. Attach the bauble to the pop-up tab.

7 Make another collage and adhere it to the back of the card. Embellish the card as desired. As shown, ribbons, gold thread, a crystal jewel, an old photo holder, and ephemera were used.

designer: jane reeves

holiday accordion card

Let someone know if they've been naughty or nice with this colorful holiday card. Use the lyrics from your favorite seasonal song to illustrate your theme. The envelope's design will easily accommodate the card's depth.

materials

Mat board

Watercolor paper or card stock
Decorative paper

Glue stick

Vellum

Photographs

Small tags, approx.
1⅛ x 1¾ inches (2.8 x 4.4 cm)

Cording or string

Self-stick hook-and-loop dots
Ribbon (optional)

Beads (optional)

Button

tools

Utility knife

Ruler

Bone folder

Scissors

Sewing needles

Sewing machine
(optional)

size:

{ 2½ x 2½ inches
(6.4 x 6.4 cm) }

process

1 Use the utility knife to cut two, 2½-inch (6.4 cm) squares from the mat board. From watercolor paper or card stock, cut or tear a strip 2¼ x 13½ inches (5.7 x 34.5 cm). Use the bone folder to score the strip at 2¼-inch (5.7 cm) intervals before folding it using the accordion fold.

2 Cut two, 3½-inch (8.9 cm) squares from decorative paper, and glue them to one side of the mat-board squares.

3 Using copies of photos and decorative papers, create a collage on one side of the accordion. Make pockets by cutting 1½-inch (3.8 cm) squares from vellum and sewing them by hand or machine to a few sections of the accordion. Create a collage on the other side of the accordion, leaving the two end sections blank.

4 Write or print the words to a favorite song and add these to the collages. Write or print additional lyrics and glue these to tags. Attach string or cording to the tags and insert them in the vellum pockets.

5 Glue the uncovered side of the mat-board squares to the ends of the accordion. For variation, glue ribbon to the back of the mat board square before attaching them to the accordion. Use the ends of the ribbon to tie a bow on the front of the card. Finish the ends of the ribbons by stringing on beads, securing them with knots.

6 Construct the envelope using the template on page 124 as your guide. Close the envelope with self-stick hook-and-loop dots, and glue a button to front.

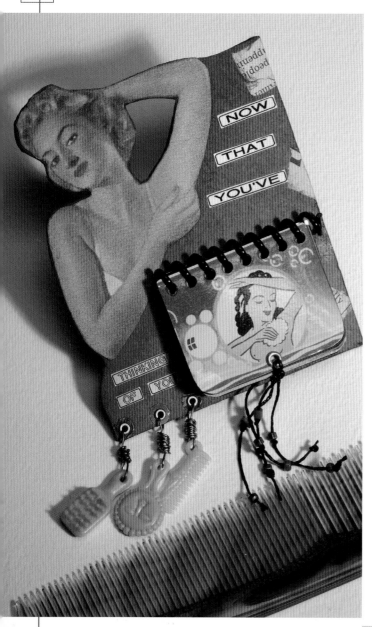

gonna wash that man

Designer Linda O'Brien made this for her very best friend at the end of her friend's relationship. Linda says, "It was the perfect assertive pick-me-up she needed at the time, and she still laughs whenever she wears the pin."

materials

Cardboard

Colorful specialty paper

Glue

Vintage photo image

Vintage deconstructed tin can

Masking tape

Eyelets

Card stock

Vintage collage material

Rubber stamps and ink

Pin back

Plastic coil

Wire

Plastic charms

Waxed linen thread

Beads

tools

Craft knife

Scissors

Tin shears

Metal hole punch

Eyelet-setting tool

Japanese screw punch or paper punch

Label maker

> size:
> Card,
> 3⅜ x 4 inches
> (8.6 x 10 cm);
> pin,
> 1½ x 2⅛ inches
> (3.8 x 5.3 cm)

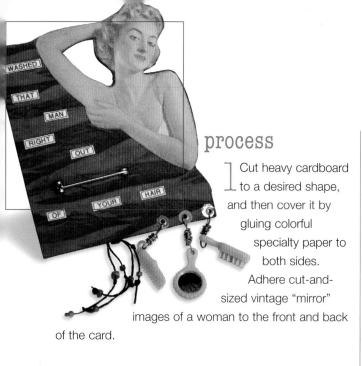

process

1. Cut heavy cardboard to a desired shape, and then cover it by gluing colorful specialty paper to both sides. Adhere cut-and-sized vintage "mirror" images of a woman to the front and back of the card.

2. Make the covers of the book from vintage tin taken from a deconstructed can. Select a can that reflects the tone of the card. Use tin shears to cut the tin to size.

3. Tape the tin covers together with masking tape so that they line up perfectly. Punch holes through the top edges to accommodate the coil. Punch holes for the closure through the center bottom edge of both covers, and set the holes with eyelets.

4. Hand punch the pages with a Japanese screw punch or paper punch so the holes line up with the holes on the covers. Collage the pages with assorted vintage advertisements, ephemera, and rubber stamps. Set aside.

5. Attach the pin back to the back cover of the book with eyelets using an eyelet-setting tool. Punch two holes in the card for attaching the pin. Add text generated by a label maker to both sides of the card. Use eyelets and an eyelet-setting tool to make three holes at the bottom left-hand corner of the card. Use the wire to attach three plastic charms.

6. Assemble your book with a coil. Make the closure by inserting waxed linen thread through the front and back closure holes. Thread the waxed linen with a few beads and knot to secure.

mini-tin albums

Keep your favorite images close at hand with tiny mini-tin albums.
Slip them in your pocket or bag for easy access any time you want
to remember friends or special times.

size:
Surf,
2½ x 1½ x ¾ inches
(6.4 x 3.8 x 1.9 cm);
Best Friends,
2¼ x 1½ x ¾ inches
(5.7 x 3.8 x 1.9 cm)

materials

Small mint tin (Surf)

Key chain mini-tin (Best Friends)

Double-sided patterned card stock

Thick white craft glue

Charms

Acrylic paint

Mini-brads

Stick-on jewels

Flower mini-embellishments

Ribbon

Stamps

Tiny safety pin

Fabric label

Embroidery floss

Decorative paper

Rubber stamps and ink

Stick-on letters

tools

Ruler

Measuring tape

Pencil

Corner rounder

Scissors

Computer and photo-editing software or photocopier

Small motorized craft tool (Surf)

designer: margert kruljac

surf
process

1. Measure the width and height of the tin. Cut double-sided patterned card stock to the width of the tin x 12 inches (30.5 cm). Measure and score the strip at intervals that are just slightly shorter than the measurement of the tin's height. Accordion fold on the scored lines. To make sure all corners of each fold will be uniform, use a corner rounder to trace around the corners before trimming them with scissors.

2. Have fun using images and embellishments to decorate the folds on one side of the strip as desired. If necessary, resize images to fit using a computer and photo-editing software or photocopier. The first image, the ocean vista, was edited with photo-editing software, which enabled the text to be printed on the image. The highlighted letters on the large metal ribbon charm—Splash—were made by painting the front of the charm with acrylic paint, and then wiping off any excess to leave paint in the engraved letters.

3. Cover the tin with decorative paper. Trace the tin lid and bottom onto patterned paper. Cut out two pieces each for the top and bottom, cutting them slightly larger than their traced outlines. Adhere one set to cover the outside of the lid and bottom, the other set to cover the insides. Measure around the sides of the lid and bottom of the tin. Cut paper accordingly and adhere. Embellish the lid with a ribbon and clasp. Use a motor-ized craft tool to drill three small holes in the upper left-hand corner of the lid. Attach the flowers by inserting brads into the drilled holes. Use stick-on letters to spell out SURF.

best friends

1. Measure the width and height of the tin. Cut double-sided patterned card stock to the height of the tin x 12 inches (30.5 cm). Measure and score the strip at intervals that are just slightly shorter than the measurement of the tin's width. Accordion fold on the scored lines. To make sure all corners of each fold will be uniform, use a corner rounder to trace around the corners before trimming them with scissors.

2. As you did for Surf, decorate one side of the strip as desired. If necessary, resize images to fit using a computer and photo-editing software or photocopier. The first page, the one that's seen when the tin is opened, was cut in half to accommodate a decorative clip-on bookmark that serves as the pull to bring the strip out of the tin. The last page has a novelty printed label attached with a safety pin. Use embroidery floss to attach tags as desired. Set the decorated strip aside.

3. Embellish the lid and add text as desired. This design does not require drilling holes in the lid. Tie various ribbons to the key chain and the stamped metal-rimmed tag.

piggyback valentine card

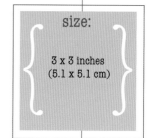

size:

3 x 3 inches
(5.1 x 5.1 cm)

When it comes to Valentine's Day, you can never say
"I love you" too many times. The tiny piggybacked card gives
you one more chance to get to the heart of the matter.

materials

Red and white card stock

White craft glue

Alphabet stickers, stamps,
or printed text*

Decorative papers

Red vellum

Narrow ribbon, ⅛ inch (.3 cm)
wide or less

Double-sided tape and/or
self-adhesive hook-and-eye
tape

tools

Paper trimmer

Ruler with metal edge

Bone folder

Heart-shaped punches,
1½-inch (3.8 cm) and ¼-inch
(.6 cm)

Scissors

*Old books are a great source
for interesting fonts

designer: jean moore

process

1 Use the paper trimmer to cut a 3- x 9-inch (5.1 x 22.9 cm) piece of red card stock.

Note: If you wish to make the card smaller or larger, trim the card stock to fit your design idea. Using the ruler and bone folder, measure and score the card at 3-inch (5.1 cm) intervals. Fold the two end panels over the middle panel, making the left-hand panel the cover of the card.

2 Use the larger heart-shaped punch to punch hearts out of the two end panels. Punch a heart out of white card stock. Set aside.

3 With scissors, cut out letters to spell words such as "Amore" and "Love," or to make longer phrases. Glue the words to the card. You may want to back the letters with bits of decorative paper. You can also use alphabet stamps or stickers to make your text.

4 Center the white punched heart on the middle panel, and glue it in place.

5 Make the border for the punched heart on the cover. Punch a heart shape from white paper, and tear around the outline. Position and glue it in place.

6 Make a tiny envelope from the red vellum. Since the envelope will be affixed to the white heart, make sure it will fit.

7 Cut a piece of card stock to make the tiny card; as shown, the size is ¾ x 1 inch (1.9 x 2.5 cm). Fold the paper in half. Glue a valentine sentiment inside the card. Use the small heart punch to punch out a red heart and glue it to the front of the card. Glue a short length of ribbon to the back of the card, which will enable you to remove the card from the envelope. Slide the card into the envelope.

8 Attach the envelope to the white heart with double-sided tape. If you want the small card to detach from the heart, use double-sided hook-and-eye tape.

Templates

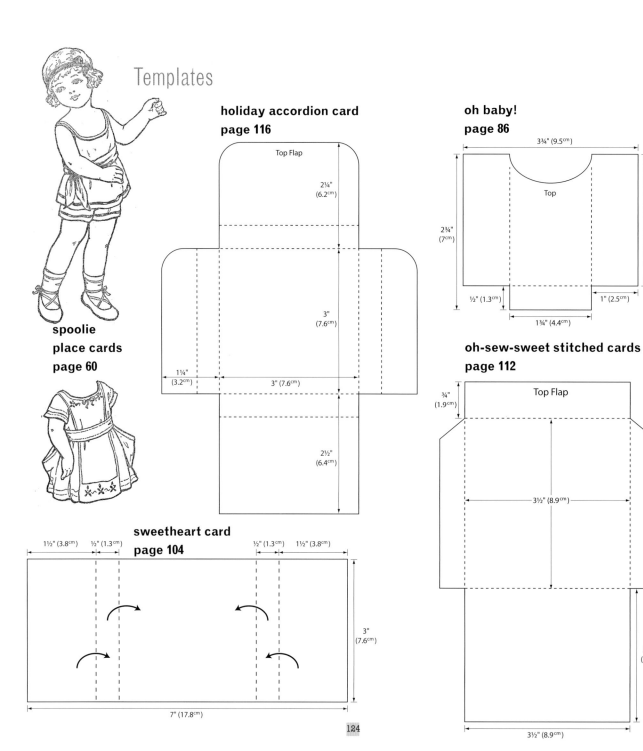

spoolie
place cards
page 60

holiday accordion card
page 116

Top Flap

2¼"
(6.2^{cm})

3"
(7.6^{cm})

1¼"
(3.2^{cm})

3" (7.6^{cm})

2½"
(6.4^{cm})

oh baby!
page 86

3¾" (9.5^{cm})

Top

2¾"
(7^{cm})

2¼"
(5.5^{cm})

½" (1.3^{cm})

1¾" (4.4^{cm})

1" (2.5^{cm})

oh-sew-sweet stitched cards
page 112

¾"
(1.9^{cm})

Top Flap

3½" (8.9^{cm})

2¾"
(7^{cm})

3½" (8.9^{cm})

sweetheart card
page 104

1½" (3.8^{cm})   ½" (1.3^{cm})   ½" (1.3^{cm})   1½" (3.8^{cm})

3"
(7.6^{cm})

7" (17.8^{cm})

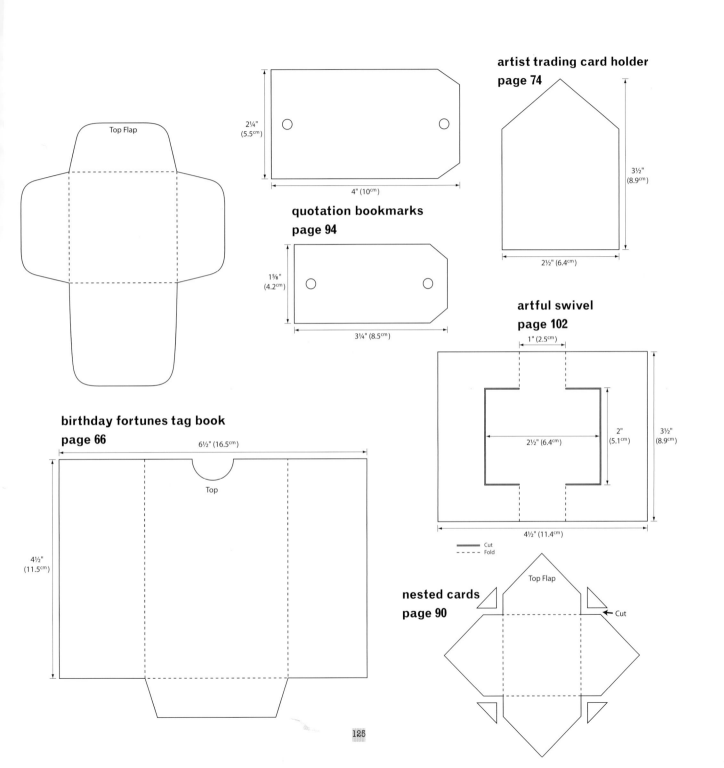

Top Flap

artist trading card holder
page 74

2¼"
(5.5ᶜᵐ)

4" (10ᶜᵐ)

3½"
(8.9ᶜᵐ)

2½" (6.4ᶜᵐ)

quotation bookmarks
page 94

1⅝"
(4.2ᶜᵐ)

3¼" (8.5ᶜᵐ)

artful swivel
page 102

1" (2.5ᶜᵐ)

2"
(5.1ᶜᵐ)

3½"
(8.9ᶜᵐ)

2½" (6.4ᶜᵐ)

4½" (11.4ᶜᵐ)

——— Cut
- - - - Fold

birthday fortunes tag book
page 66

6½" (16.5ᶜᵐ)

Top

4½"
(11.5ᶜᵐ)

nested cards
page 90

Top Flap

← Cut

Contributing Designers

Sandra Evertson Austin, Texas
Sandra is the author of several books, among them *Fanciful Paper Flowers* (Lark/Chapelle, 2006). She is a frequent contributor to *Stampington* and other craft publications. She has a large cat, Romeo, and a tiny dog, Juliet. You can see more of her work at her website www.ParisFleaMarketDesigns.com

Kim Grant Chanhassen, Minnesota
Kim is a nationally represented artist and international instructor working in mixed water media and collage. Her work is found in numerous corporate and private collections. Visit her website at www.kimgrantdesigns.com.

Anne Igou Las Vegas, Nevada
Anne is a leading artist and designer of both polymer clay and semi-precious jewelry. Her techniques can be seen in magazines and craft shows on the HGTV and DIY Networks. You can visit her website at www.blushingmarie.com.

Margert Kruljac Hinton, West Virginia
Margert is a freelance artist dabbling in scrapbooking and altered art. She designs for manufacturers, teaches around the country, and has been published numerous times in popular craft magazines. She lives with her husband and two children in the scenic mountains of West Virginia.

Claudia Lee Liberty, Tennessee
Claudia Lee is a full-time studio artist, instructor and author. She livesin Middle Tennessee where she runs Liberty Paper Mill, a working and teaching facility. You can contact her at paperlee@dtccom.net.

Susan McBride Asheville, North Carolina
Susan is an art director, illustrator, and author of the children's book, *The Don't-Get-Caught Doodle Notebook* (Lark, 2005). Her work has appeared in many Lark books including, *Altered Art, Artful Cards*, and *Making Creative Journals*.

Nicole McConville Asheville, North Carolina
Nicole is an artist with an interest in correspondence art, collage, and assemblage. View more of her work at www.sigilation.com.

Jean Tomaso Moore Asheville, North Carolina
Jean is a mixed-media artist who has created many projects for Lark Books. She lives in Asheville with her guitarist husband, Richard. You can contact her at LeaningTowerArt@msn.com.

Nikki-Shell (Nicola Prested) Melbourne, Australia
Nicola is a Brit girl living her dream in Australia with husband Kev and two little chicks, Mia and Esme. She loves anything crafty, but admits to a particular love for sewing and knitting. Whenever possible, she tries to use recycled materials. You can find her at her blog www.nikkishell.typepad.com.

Opie and Linda O'Brien North Perry Village, Ohio
Opie and Linda are mixed-media artists, authors, and teachers who consider themselves "caretakers of the mundane and the ordinary." They use organic, recycled, and found materials in their work. Their unique offerings include jewelry, dolls, books, assemblage, collage, masks, and more. You can visit their website at www.burntofferings.com.

Jane Powell Saluda, North Carolina
Jane Powell moved from Chicago to the quiet mountain town of Saluda, NC, in 1994. Her shop on main street, Random Arts, offers supplies for crafters and artists. Visit her website at www.randomartsnow.com

Jane Reeves Black Mountain, North Carolina
Jane Reeves makes quilts, collages, and mixed media constructions. Her work is included in corporate and private collections and has been shown at Quilt National.

Angela Richardson Madison, Wisconsin
Angela leads a dynamic creative life as a visual artist andperformer. In the studio, she works primarily with paper to create collage, utilizing both cut-and-paste and stitched methods. Learn more about her work at www.caculo.com/angela/.

Chris Schwartz St. Louis Missouri
Chris Schwartz and her sister, designer Sharon Wisely, own Red Lead, a paper arts and rubber stamp store in St. Louis, MO. On any given day, you can find Chris in the store doing what she loves best—stamping, collaging, and preparing to teach one of her weekly worksohps or demos. You can keep up with Read Lead on their blog at www.readlead.typepad.com/, or visit their webstore at www.redleadpaperworks.com.

Molly Smith Benbrook, Texas
Molly, a native Texan, is a craft designer specializing in paper quilling. In addition to designing for a major company in the craft industry, she contributes to various books and magazines. She is the author of *The New Paper Quilling* (Lark Books, 2006). Her website is at www.amytree.com.

Jen Swearington Asheville, North Carolina
Jen is the creator of Jennythreads silk clothing and accessories. She is formally trained in the fine arts and textiles. Her work can be found at www.jennythreads.net.

Terry Taylor Asheville, North Carolina
Terry is a recognized jeweler and mixed media artist. He is the author of several Lark books including *Altered Art* (2004), *Artful Paper Dolls* (2006), and *The Altered Object* (2007).

Mary Teichman Florence, Massachusetts
Mary studied calligraphy at the Cooper Union School of Art in New York City, where she received her BFA. She is a printmaker, illustrator, and painter. Her etchings are in the collections of the Brooklyn Museum, The Museum of the City of New York, The Corcoran Museum and the National Museum of Women in the Arts. Visit her website at www.mtcalligraphy.com.

Karen Timm Madison, Wisconsin
Karen is a paper, fiber, and book artist. Her passions include using papers from around the world and mixing a variety of fabrics, to create 3-D fiber art pieces or artist books. You can see her work at www.winnebagostudios.com

Luann Udell Keene, New Hampshire
Luann is a nationally exhibited mixed-media artist and jewelry maker. She creates fiber collage assemblages with her own handmade polymer clay artifacts. She is the author of *Rubber Stamp Carving* (Lark Books, 2002). See more of her work at her website: www.durable-goods.com.

Hope Wallace Owings Mills, Maryland
Hope can often be found roaming antiques shops for old photos, Victorian era magazines, and other ephemera. She works in both cut-and-paste and digital collage, depending on her mood and the piece. For more information visit www.paperrelics.com.

Sharon Wisely St. Louis, Missouri
Sharon describes herself as a "combination collage," since stitching, cutting paper, painting, and stamping—all patched together—are what she does best! She loves every minute of minding her paper arts store, Red Lead (along with sister Chris Schwartz), in St. Louis, MO. You can visit her blog at www.cut-up paper.typepad.com, and the store website at www.redleadpaperworks.com.

Index